W9-AXE-170

# Frommer's®

# Yosemite
### A N D
# Sequoia/Kings Canyon National Parks

**1st Edition**

**by Stacey Wells**

Macmillan • USA

## About the Author

Stacey Wells is a native Californian who grew up in the foothills of the Sierra Nevada before relocating to the Bay Area. She currently lives in Oakland, where she is a newspaper reporter and freelance writer.

## MACMILLAN TRAVEL

A Simon & Schuster Macmillan Company
1633 Broadway
New York, NY 10019

Find us online at **www.frommers.com**

ISBN 0-02-862055-0
ISSN 1093-9814

Editor: Bob O'Sullivan
Production Editor: Michael Thomas
Production Team: Eric Brinkman, David Faust, Heather Pope, and Karen Teo
Design by Michele Laseau
Digital Cartography by Roberta Stockwell and Ortelius Design

## SPECIAL SALES

Bulk purchases (10+ copies) of Frommer's and selected Macmillan travel guides are available to corporations, organizations, mail-order catalogs, institutions, and charities at special discounts, and can be customized to suit individual needs. For more information write to Special Sales, Macmillan General Reference, 1633 Broadway, New York, NY 10019.

# Contents

# List of Maps

Line drawings on pages 147, 148 (sugar pine), 149, 150, 151, 152 (lupine, cow parsnip, yarrow), 153, 154, 155, 156, 157, 158, 159, 160, 161 (western tanager, belted kingfisher), 162, 163, 164, 165, 167, 168, 169, and 170 (grey fox, bobcat, mountain lion) © Giselle Simons.

Line drawings on pages 148 (lodgepole pine), 152 (monkey flower), 161 (American dipper), 166, and 170 (coyote, black bear) © Jasper Burns.

## AN INVITATION TO THE READER

In researching this book, we discovered many wonderful places—hotels, restaurants, shops, and more. We're sure you'll find others. Please tell us about them so that we can share the information with your fellow travelers in upcoming editions. If you were disappointed with a recommendation, we'd love to know that, too. Please write to:

*Frommer's Guide to Yosemite and Sequoia/
Kings Canyon National Parks*
Macmillan Travel
1633 Broadway
New York, NY 10019

## AN ADDITIONAL NOTE

Please be advised that travel information is subject to change at any time. The publisher and the author have endeavored to provide useful information in this publication, but we suggest that you write or call ahead for confirmation when making your travel plans. The publisher and author cannot be held responsible for the experiences of readers while traveling. National parks are, by their very nature, potentially hazardous places. In visiting any of the places or doing any of the activities described herein, readers assume all risk of injury or loss that may accompany such activities. The publisher and the author disavow all responsibility for injury, death, loss, or property damage that may arise from a reader's visit to any of the places or participation in any of the activities described herein, and the publisher and the author make no warranties regarding the competence, safety, and reliability of outfitters, tour companies, or training centers described in this publication.

## WHAT THE SYMBOLS MEAN
### ✪ Frommer's Favorites

Our favorite places and experiences—outstanding for quality, value, or both.

The following abbreviations are used for credit cards:

| | | | |
|---|---|---|---|
| AE | American Express | EU | Eurocard |
| CB | Carte Blanche | JCB | Japan Credit Bank |
| DC | Diners Club | MC | MasterCard |
| DISC | Discover | V | Visa |

## FIND FROMMER'S ONLINE

Arthur Frommer's Outspoken Encyclopedia of Travel (www.frommers.com) offers more than 6,000 pages of up-to-the-minute travel information—including the latest bargains and candid, personal articles updated daily by Arthur Frommer himself. No other web site offers such comprehensive and timely coverage of the world of travel.

# Introduction to Yosemite & Sequoia/Kings Canyon National Parks

$C$alifornia's Sierra Nevada region imposes rugged features on a state many associate with sandy beaches and palm trees. It's a mountain range of great beauty hidden amid harsh wilderness, and nowhere is the terrain more dramatic than in Yosemite and Sequoia/Kings Canyon national parks. Both combine mountains with meadows, waterfalls with wildflowers, and spectacular geology with awe-inspiring vistas that span, in some cases, nearly across the breadth of the state. Together, these parks cover 1.6 million acres (roughly 2,520 square miles). They host approximately 6 million visitors a year and are home to thousands of species of plants and animals.

The bigger tourist attraction of the two parks is Yosemite, and it's no wonder why. Yosemite covers 1,169 square miles—roughly the size of Rhode Island—and 94% is designated wilderness. In the span of a mile here, you can behold the quiet beauty of a forest, walk into a pristine meadow, observe a sunset from a towering granite cliff, hike a half-mile-high waterfall, enjoy a moonlit night as bright as day, climb a rock, and eat a gourmet meal before falling asleep, be it under the stars or in a luxurious bed in a four-star hotel.

Yosemite Valley, where 95% of tourists head, is just a small sliver of the park, but it holds the bulk of the region's jaw-dropping features. An estimated 4.1 million people visit here each year. It is a place of record-setting statistics: the highest waterfall in North America and three of the tallest in the world (Upper Yosemite, Sentinel and Ribbon falls); the biggest and tallest piece of exposed granite (El Capitan); and stands of the Giant Sequoia.

Wawona is a 30-minute drive south of the valley. It's a small community that was annexed to the park in 1932. Wawona is mostly a hodgepodge of resort cabins and private homes, but it's also home to the stately Wawona Hotel, a nine-hole golf course, and its main

# Yosemite National Park

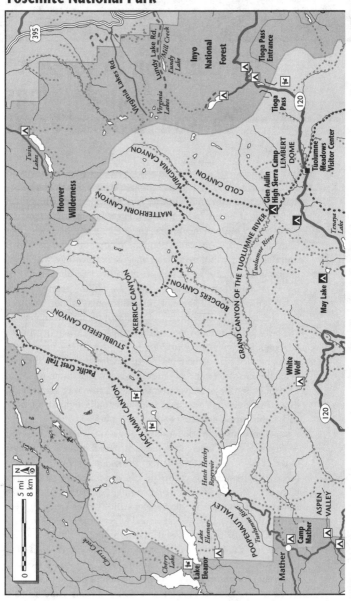

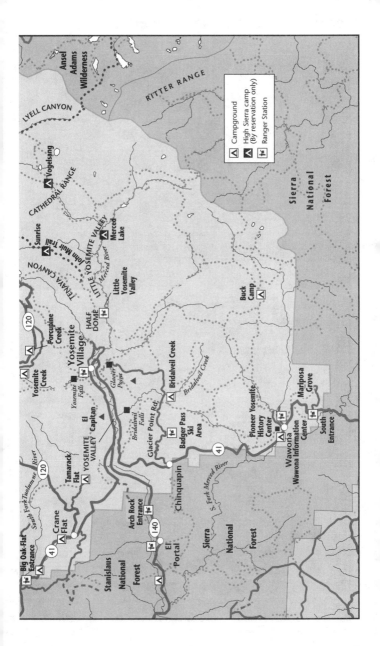

# Sequoia & Kings Canyon National Parks

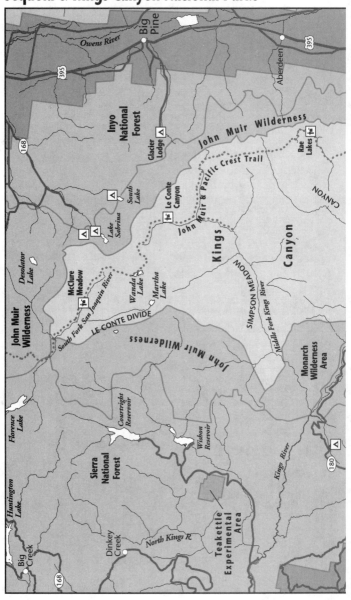

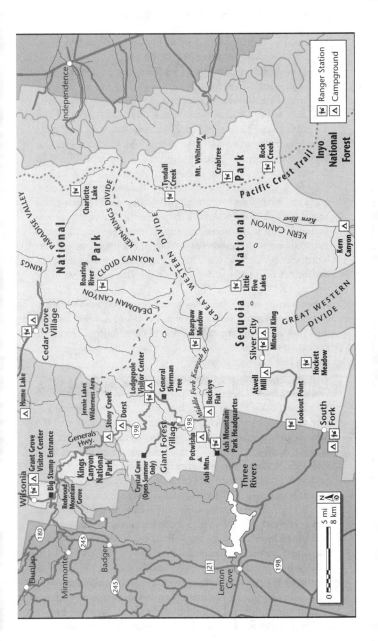

5

attraction—the Mariposa Grove of Big Trees, a stand of Giant Sequoias that tower between 200 and 300 feet tall.

An hour northeast of the valley lies Tuolumne Meadows, an immense plateau dotted with wildflowers and the glimmering Tuolumne River. It is surrounded by a half-dozen domes and peaks. The high country also includes White Wolf Lodge, Tenaya and Tioga lakes, and Tuolumne Lodge. The two lodges are little more than restaurants with a collection of tent-cabins. All of these, plus backcountry outposts accessible only on foot, are described in chapter 5.

In the heart of the Sierra Nevada, just south of Yosemite, are Sequoia and Kings Canyon national parks, home to the largest Giant Sequoia trees in the world and a deep gorge of a canyon that rivals Yosemite Valley. Sequoia and Kings Canyon are separate parks snuggled next to one another and managed as a single entity. Combined, they outsize Yosemite. Peaks stretch across 1,350 square miles and include the 14,494-foot Mount Whitney, the tallest point in the continental United States. These parks are also home to the Kaweah Range, a string of dark, beautiful mountains nestled amid the Sierra and three powerful rivers: the Kings, Kern, and Kaweah. Despite their size, these parks attract less than half the number of Yosemite's annual visitors, making them an appreciated alternative for those looking to avoid huge crowds.

## 1  History of the Region

This region of the Sierra Nevada has a rich natural and cultural history. The landscape can change completely from one mile to the next. High mountain meadows give way to turbulent rivers that thunder down deep gorges, tumble over vast waterfalls, and turn into wide, shallow rivers as they meander through the next valley. Such diversity can be attributed to the region's geologic roots, which stretch back between 10 and 80 million years ago when a head-on collision between two immense plates of rock formed this mountain range. The rock, weakened by extreme temperature variations, was later carved by erosion into deep valleys, including Yosemite Valley and Kings Canyon. In a process described more fully in chapter 9, the Ice Age brought glaciers that smoothed the faces of rocks such as Yosemite's El Capitan and Half Dome, as well as some of the towering peaks of Yosemite's Tuolumne Meadows and the Kings Canyon.

Long after the ice melted but before the United States got hot on preservation, all this land was home to a handful of Indian tribes.

These were people who cared deeply about protecting their tribal lands, and there are quite a few stories of bloody confrontations in these mountains. But war was never waged for plunder or honor; old-fashioned revenge sparked most of the violence.

Native Americans were aware of Yosemite at least 5,000 years ago. While much of the world lay in darkness and Egyptian scholars were making their first use of numbers, Indians in California were living as their forebears had for thousands of years. By 1000 B.C., there were tribes—namely the Ahwahneeches (Ah-wah'-nee-ches), a subtribe of the Miwok, living in Yosemite Valley. Archaeologists have since documented 36 living sites on the valley floor that supported a vast number of inhabitants with its lush fauna and vegetation. The largest village lay just below Yosemite Falls.

The Ahwahneeches were fantastic storytellers. Living amid towering cliffs, strangely shaped rocks, and dozens of waterfalls, they spun tales to explain the creation of the natural wonders that surrounded them. Almost every landmark in today's parks has a story, several of which are included in this book.

Despite the fact that the early inhabitants were called Ahwahneeches, the valley was named Yosemite by a bunch of angry white guys. They were Yosemite's first tourists—soldiers sent to oust Native American tribes who refused to relocate to the Plains. While seated around a campfire, a doctor among the group suggested the soldiers settle upon a name for the valley. Among the suggestions were Paradise Valley and Yosemite, the name by which the Indian tribes in the region were known. Some were offended by the suggestion to honor Native Americans in the valley, but in the end Yosemite won. Unfortunately, Yosemite was the soldiers' mispronunciation of the word *Oo-hoo-ma-te,* the name of just one settlement of Ahwahneeches in the valley. The Oohoomate were great hunters of grizzly bears and the word *Oohoomate* translates roughly to "killers among us." Soldiers drove the Ahwahneeches out of the valley in 1851.

South of the Ahwahneeches lived the neighboring Monaches, who met their fate during the smallpox outbreak in 1862. The Monaches, also known as the Western Monos, lived in Kings Canyon. This tribe was a subgroup of the Paiute Indians, who lived east of the Sierra Nevada near Mono Lake and migrated westward over the mountain range. The Monaches kept villages in the foothills all year long, although sometimes moved to the forest in the summer. The Potwishas and Wuksachis were subgroups of the Monaches, who also lived in the foothills, around Sequoia's Ash Mountain. In today's park, there's a campground called Potwisha and a motel under construction that will be named Wuksachi.

Kings Canyon was named in 1806 by a Spaniard, Gabriel Moraga, the first European to lead an expedition in these parts. The party discovered a major river on January 6, the Roman Catholic day of the Epiphany. Being a good Catholic, Moraga christened the river El Rio de los Santos Reyes, or "the river of the holy kings" in honor of the three wise men who visited the infant Jesus on the same date. The name was later shortened to Kings River.

The land of Kings Canyon and Sequoia remained obscure until 1827, when trappers arrived. The California Gold Rush drew hoards more in 1849 and abandoned mines dot Sequoia and Kings Canyon national parks, especially in Mineral King, a region unsuccessfully mined for silver in the 1800s.

Perhaps it was a combination of prehistoric earthquakes, glaciers, smallpox, and fortune-seekers that made survivors out of Yosemite, Sequoia, and Kings Canyon. Each park was destined for destruction (and some argue that Yosemite has been destroyed—by tourism). But we're talking about heavy-duty stuff: dams, logging, flooding. Large stands of Giant Sequoia were obliterated in the late 1800s. Ranchers allowed their sheep to graze beneath the big trees. Sawmills were built nearby and zip-zip, down came entire forests. Adding insult to injury is the fact that the wood of the largest Giant Sequoias is pretty useless. It breaks across the grain, is brittle, and shatters when the trees thunder to the ground. Nevertheless, early loggers chopped down a third of the ancient trees in the region. The wood was used to make wooden stakes for vineyards and pencils. This travesty would likely have continued if not for a few mid-19th-century conservationists, who pushed to turn the areas into parks. In 1890, Sequoia National Park was created, along with the tiny General Grant National Park, established to protect Grant Grove. But the move was too late to spare the Converse Basin. Once the largest stand of Giant Sequoias in the world, today it's a cemetery of tree stumps, the grave markers of fallen giants.

In 1926, the park was expanded eastward to include the smaller Kern Canyon and Mount Whitney. But rumblings continued over the fate of the Kings Canyon itself. For a while, its future lie as a reservoir. It wasn't until the 1960s that Kings Canyon was finally protected for good. In 1978, Mineral King was added to Sequoia's half of the park, and since then the boundaries have stayed put. The parks have been managed jointly since World War II.

While the fight to save the Giant Sequoias raged, a similar battle was taking place to spare Yosemite. Here the threat came from opportunists hoping to cash in on Yosemite Valley's beauty. Soon after the Ahwahneeches were driven out, homesteaders came in. They built hotels and crude homes and planted row crops and orchards. Somehow Congress convinced President Abraham Lincoln during the Civil War to sign legislation protecting the valley and the nearby Mariposa Grove of Giant Sequoias. This was the first time the federal government had reached out to protect land in perpetuity. So Yosemite Valley was, in effect, the first state and national park in America. But thousands of acres surrounding these relatively small holdings were still subject to exploitation. Mining, logging, and grazing were devastating the nearby wilderness. On October 1, 1890, a week after approving Sequoia National Park, Congress established Yosemite National Park. The new park did not include the valley or Mariposa Grove, but encompassed enormous tracts of surrounding wilderness. The original boundaries of the park were 25% larger than today.

With two administrations—one overseeing the valley and big trees and one for the park—some overlap occurred and frustration mounted. In 1906, legislation added the valley and big trees to the park in exchange for reducing its size to follow more natural contours in the land while excluding private mining and logging operations. Everyone was set to live happily ever after. No one would have predicted that Yosemite would become one of the most popular places on the planet.

Recent years have brought a disquieting sense of foreboding to this wilderness haven. One trip during peak season and you'll understand why. Traffic backs up for miles, trees and branches along the Merced River become clotheslines, and candy wrappers, cigarette butts, and paper products litter the valley. The songbirds can barely be heard over the din of voices yelling and hooting as if each were Grizzly Adams and this valley were their own private conquest. At times like these, New York's Central Park offers more respite. This is the biggest challenge facing Yosemite today, and to a far lesser extent, Sequoia and Kings Canyon. Big changes are expected in the next 5 years as the Park Service grapples with the best way to permit access without causing more irreparable damage to this natural wonderland.

Who would have thought that preservation would wreak its own brand of havoc here? We can only imagine how this beautiful place would appear today had it been left in the hands of profiteers.

## 2   The Parks Today

In Yosemite, recent rock slides and torrential flooding have forever changed the park's appearance, but the human influence has wreaked much more havoc in the past 2 decades than Mother Nature. About 4 million people visit Yosemite a year—in the summer, the average daily census hits 20,000 (attendance has doubled in the last 20 years)! The major difficulty facing park officials today, due to this increasing popularity, is balancing access to Yosemite's wonders with what's healthy to preserve the park. So, here's how things stand now: Just prior to publication of this book, the National Park Service issued a 10-year master plan aimed at reducing vehicle traffic in Yosemite Valley. The full plan may take up to a decade to implement and will severely limit day access to the park. The idea is to eventually ban all day-use vehicles from the valley. You would then drive to a staging area, park the car in a huge lot, and board a tour bus. Once in the valley, the shuttle service would be visitors' sole source of transport. Overnight guests in the valley could still drive in, but would be required to park their cars and use the shuttle. Drivers could still go it alone to reach Wawona or Tuolumne Meadows. Many who love Yosemite say this is a small price to pay to protect a treasure.

It's a far different scenario at Sequoia and Kings Canyon national parks. These too get crowded in summer, when RVs and slow drivers can cause a convoy dozens of cars long—but it's nothing like Yosemite. Sequoia and Kings Canyon are much less developed, and what is developed is much more spread out. Frankly, officials here have learned a lesson from Yosemite and work hard not to make the same mistakes. The park is beautiful, with gorgeous canyons and some of the most spectacular trees and vistas in the Sierra, but they are not all crammed into a 7-mile valley and you won't find a crowd three deep jostling for a view.

Crowds aside, there's a movement at both Yosemite and Sequoia/Kings Canyon to return the parks to a more natural state. Not only does this require restoring nature, but to some extent, ensuring that manmade elements introduced into the park reflect and work with the surroundings. Nowhere is this more evident than in Yosemite Valley, where Mother Nature is forcing officials to make changes long planned but never implemented. For the past 20 years, Yosemite National Park had been governed in part by a general plan that called for restoring meadows, phasing out some campgrounds, and moving others away from waterways to reduce the human impact on rivers, streams, and wildlife. However, little progress had been made. Then in January 1997, during one of the valley's swanky annual winter events, Mother Nature retaliated.

What began as a torrential downpour turned into one of the worst winter storms on record, and when the rain stopped several days later Yosemite Valley was Yosemite lake. Swollen streams and creeks swept tons of debris—trees, rocks, brush—into the valley, clogging the Merced River. Campgrounds were submerged, employees' quarters flooded, and much of Yosemite Lodge was under 2 feet of water. Despite frantic attempts at sandbagging, hundreds of people were forced onto higher ground—the top floor of buildings—and everyone was stuck. The water was so high and ferocious that it washed out roads and stranded about 2,000 people in the valley, including the several hundred on hand to celebrate New Year's Eve. So much was damaged that the valley closed for almost 3 months, and even after it reopened travel was restricted on the park's all-weather highway.

Even now, a year later, much remains lost. While park workers managed to clean most of the fallen trees, boulders, and rocks out of heavily-populated areas in the valley by mid-1997, some backcountry trail bridges remain unrepaired, and almost half of the campsites in the valley are gone. The same series of storms also wreaked havoc to the south, in Sequoia and Kings Canyon national parks. The only two access roads were buried beneath mud slides and rising rivers. Pelting rain caused 100 landslides on the Generals Highway. Highway 180 was submerged along a 12-mile stretch that winds along the south fork of the Kings River between Grant and Cedar groves. When the water receded, the road had collapsed in a half-dozen places, in some sections up to a mile long.

The storms remind us all of the history behind both parks. Millions of years of water, snow, and glaciers have carved the unique canyons of Yosemite Valley and Kings Canyon. So the folks who live here do so with a measure of understanding: They're living at the mercy of Mother Nature.

Before the winter of '97 turned everyone's priorities topsy-turvy, officials at both Yosemite and Sequoia/Kings Canyon were already on their way to making some other notable changes. Both parks are renovating and reconstructing. Countless meadows in Yosemite are off-limits to foot traffic so that grass and wildflowers can return. Work was just completed on several new eateries, including the new Mountain Room Restaurant, which looks out at Yosemite Falls. A new gift store that doubles during the winter as a cross-country ski lodge has also just opened at Glacier Point. In both cases, new structures replaced existing ones, so the impact on pristine wilderness was minimal. Floor-to-ceiling windows bring the outdoors inside. There are plans to continue whittling down accommodations at Yosemite's Curry Village, the valley's low-rent district. And park officials say they will eventually relocate the campgrounds lost in 1997 to higher ground away from the riverbanks. In addition, horses are no longer available in Yosemite Valley, although arrangements can be made to transport and board your own livestock if necessary. See chapter 3.

In Sequoia/Kings Canyon, park officials are putting the finishing touches on a 16-year sequoia forest restoration project. Most of the details will affect Giant Forest, one of the most notable stands of trees in Sequoia National Park. The project calls for tearing down old buildings and moving parking lots and roads. The goal is ecological restoration—an ambitious plan to return this area of the park to what it might have been had buildings never been built. The idea is not that visitors will like the new digs more than the existing kitschy buildings, but to cease damaging the sequoias' root systems, repair the topsoil, plant sequoia seedlings, and get out of the way while Mother Nature does her thing.

Another important item on the Sequoia/Kings Canyon agenda these days is to move folks away from falling trees and branches. Not that they have a huge propensity for falling, but eventually they do—and when one of these mammoths topples over, it can take out a small town. In 1940, a tree smashed the home of the then–park superintendent who was, thankfully, away. A visitor was killed in 1969 when a branch came careening down. And in 1992, two huge trees came crashing down near the Giant Forest Lodge. Needless to say, the lodge folks want to move as soon as possible.

So, the big news on this front is that all commercial enterprise in the Giant Forest portion of the park will be evacuated by the fall of 1998. Lodging and food services are scheduled for restoration at the new Wuksachi Village by the year 2001. Whether those timetables will be met remains to be seen, but it would be a good idea to keep it in mind while planning your trip. In addition, there are plans to limit vehicle access to some trees in the Giant Forest grove.

Interestingly, park officials also hope that natural fires will return to the area once the human influence is gone. Fires are an important part of the sequoia's life. The bark of the giant trees is fire resistant, but a blaze will dry out the sequoia's cones, which then open, dropping seeds onto the the fire-cleared ground, which is the preferred growth medium for seedlings. The heavy commercial influence in the Giant Forest has impeded this process. Fire suppression actually proves more of a hazard, because without fire, brush and dead wood pile up, providing extra fuel should a blaze begin. Extra fuel increases a fire's temperature and intensifies its behavior, allowing it to permanently damage or even kill mature trees.

In these parks, preserving nature was once an afterthought. Rangers used to toss burning logs down from Yosemite Valley's tall cliffs, bear feeds at the Sequoia/Kings Canyon dump were a huge attraction for visitors, and there was little attention paid to keeping things as is and more attention given to making things more bizarre than they already were. Thankfully, that time has passed and today's visitors know from the get-go that even the simplest pine cones and ordinary river rocks are crucial to the park's environment.

## 3  The Best of Yosemite & Sequoia/Kings Canyon

It's hard to pick the best of anything, and especially hard when nature is at hand. There are so many heart-thumping hikes, roaring waterfalls, and mind-blowing vistas to explore in these parks, it's almost impossible to pick our favorites. That being said, we're ready with a few suggestions. Here goes:

### THE BEST VIEWS

**The Panorama from Tunnel View Outside Yosemite Valley**    If you're coming to the park on Highway 41 from Wawona, this amazing panorama will sneak up on you, offering a breathtaking surprise. There's plenty of space here to pull over and look. See chapter 3.

**Yosemite Valley from Glacier Point**    The easy drive to the top will leave you speechless. From here, you'll get an eye-level view of great rocks such as Half Dome, North Dome, and Cloud's Rest and the valley and waterfalls looming far below. See chapter 3.

**Mist Falls from the Bottom in Kings Canyon**    Standing at the base of this waterfall, you'll really appreciate its force, especially during spring and early summer when it's fed by the snowmelt. The crashing of water onto the rocks below drowns out all other noise, and there are rainbows galore. Keep back from the slippery rocks at its edge! See chapter 6.

### THE BEST CAR CAMPGROUNDS

**North Pines Campground in Yosemite Valley**    Smaller and slightly more isolated than neighboring camps, it's the most enjoyable of the three car campgrounds in the valley. They also have a no pets policy (it's not that we don't love Fido, but when you're traveling petless, camping near someone else's dog only makes you homesick). See chapter 5.

**Buckeye Flat Campground in Sequoia**    This is a small campground situated in the foothills, where it can get very hot in the summer, but its location amid a grove of oaks is especially pretty and secluded. See chapter 8.

**Sunset Campground in Kings Canyon**    Situated over a rolling hilltop beneath tall trees, this is a peaceful place that glows late into the evening as the sun goes down. It offers some nicely secluded sights, and it's in a good location to hike to some really big trees. See chapter 8.

## THE BEST PRIMITIVE CAMPGROUNDS

**Yosemite Creek**    Just outside Yosemite Valley on Highway 120, you'll find this great out-of-the-way campground that lacks amenities. It is far enough off the beaten path to offer solitude. Few venture down the dirt road to this campground and those who do tend to prefer roughing it. See chapter 5.

**South Fork Campground in Sequoia**    This is the smallest developed campsite in the park. It's just inside the park's boundary, set at 3,650 feet along the south fork of the beautiful Kaweah River. See chapter 8.

**Atwell Mill Campground in Sequoia**    The site is situated along Atwell Creek near the east fork of the Kaweah River in the Mineral King region of the park. You need time and patience to reach it, but it's well worth it. See chapter 8.

## THE BEST DAY HIKES

**Vernal Fall in Yosemite**    A must-see for anyone with the stamina. It's just 3 miles round-trip if you follow the Mist Trail, but it requires a strong heart and enough gumption to make the last quarter-mile, ascending 500 stairs. Once at the top, hikers are rewarded with fabulous views, swimming holes, and enough space to lounge around before the hike back down. See chapter 4.

**Moro Rock in Sequoia**    A short but steep climb up a historic staircase that snakes through rock crevices to the top of Moro Rock. Rewards include one of the most awe-inspiring views in the Sierra Nevada. The walk offers plenty of places to rest on the way up. See chapter 7.

**Mist Falls in Kings Canyon**   This 8-mile hike climbs 1,500 feet to the spectacular Mist Falls. Along the way, hiking ranges from moderately strenuous to easy strolls through woodland areas that have lots of resting places. See chapter 7.

## THE BEST ACCESSIBLE HIGH COUNTRY DESTINATIONS

**May Lake in Yosemite**   This is an easy 2.5-mile hike that begins near Highway 120, east of White Wolf. This picturesque walk offers fishing but no swimming. May Lake is dead center in Yosemite National Park. It's a good place to survey surrounding peaks, including the 10,855-foot-high Mt. Hoffman that rises behind the lake. See chapter 4.

**The High Sierra Trail in Sequoia**   This popular backpacking trail offers day hikers a glimpse of just what's out there. It's a moderate hike with pretty views of the middle fork of the Kaweah River and the Kaweah Range. See chapter 7.

**Paradise Valley in Kings Canyon**   This hike extends beyond Mist Falls to a broad valley bisected by a welcoming river. It's a long 14-mile round-trip hike to do in 1 day, but it is possible with some planning and an early start. See chapter 7.

## THE BEST WATERFALLS

**Yosemite Falls in Yosemite Valley**   Oh, we're going to get in trouble for this one. How can one choose, with so many sparkling waterfalls in the vicinity? Well, it's like choosing a diamond. This one's bigger. It falls farther, makes more noise, gets people wetter, and in winter forms a huge snowcone at its base, sometimes reaching 300 feet high. Sadly, it's usually all dried up by late summer. See chapter 3.

**Mist Falls in Kings Canyon**   A winner on a couple of fronts. There aren't that many waterfalls in Sequoia/Kings Canyon, and this one is the prettiest. Seeing it requires a hike, but don't stop until you reach the sign identifying the falls because the first waterfall is a decoy. The real thing is much more breathtaking. See chapter 6.

## THE BEST ROCK

**El Capitan in Yosemite Valley**   Half Dome's more unusual and distinctive, but it also gets all the attention. El Capitan on the other hand gets far too little. Look at this rock and think about this: It is the largest single piece of exposed granite *and* its shape defies gravity by slanting slightly outward near the top. Still, people climb all over it. During the day you'll see rock climbers and at night you'll see their flashlights strung across the face like erratic Christmas tree lights. See chapter 3.

## THE BEST TREE

**The Lincoln Tree in Sequoia**    It's hard to say why. There are so many big, beautiful conifers. Some are taller, some are wider. This one just looks perfect. Kind of stately, kind of humble, standing on its own away from the crowd. See chapter 7.

## THE BEST PICNIC SPOTS

**Sentinel Beach in Yosemite Valley**    A short walk from just about everywhere, the picnic area is away from valley central and the accompanying congestion. There are picnic tables, and access to the Merced River is easy. A nice trail leads back to Yosemite Lodge. See chapter 3.

**South Fork of the Kaweah River Below Mist Falls in Kings Canyon**    Take the hike to Mist Falls and after the first steep ascent the river will be visible on your left. For the next half-mile or so, before you can see the main fall, there are myriad places to pull aside for a picnic. See chapter 8.

## THE BEST MEALS

**Ahwahnee Dining Room in Yosemite Valley**    No surprise here. It's a knockout feast. Every course is almost worth its weight in gold, which is about what it'll cost you, too. See chapter 5.

**Wawona Hotel Dining Room**    Take a step back in time by traveling south of Yosemite Valley to this hotel (nice in its own right) and dining room, where the food is considered another of nature's treasures. See chapter 5.

## THE BEST AFFORDABLE MEALS

**Curry Village Pizza Patio**    The food's edible, adults and kids love it, and there's soda and beer on tap. Grab a chair outside on the deck, kick back, and watch the sea of humanity stroll by. See chapter 5.

**Grant Grove Coffee Shop in Kings Canyon**    A light-fare menu includes enough variety to please everyone. This beats the cafeterias, both in terms of cost and quality. See chapter 8.

## THE BEST PLACES TO STOCK UP ON SUPPLIES

**Village Store in Yosemite Valley**    It's a small grocery that also sells those forgotten articles, flashlights, batteries, tarp, etc. None of the costs mirror prices you'd find in the real world, but it's the only option that doesn't involve driving 40 miles. The one exception: The wine selection at the market in Curry Village looks a little better. See chapter 5.

**Lodgepole Market Center in Sequoia**    Ditto, although there are markets throughout the park that carry pretty much the same stuff. The real benefit here is location. It's near a post office, laundry, and other amenities you or the kids may find yourselves missing. See chapter 8.

## THE BEST PLACES TO TAKE THE KIDS

**Happy Isles Nature Center in Yosemite Valley**    A natural wonderland laid out at a child's eye level. The nature center, recently renovated, can entertain kids for hours with exhibits, ranger talks, and enough outdoor space to zoom around. See chapter 3.

**Walter Fry Nature Center in Sequoia**    Located at the Lodgepole Campground, this is a fun place for children to visit during the summer months. They can look through a microscope, watch water bugs, and generally get entrained, albeit briefly. See chapter 6.

## THE BEST PLACES FOR REFLECTION

**Yosemite's Glacier Point at Night**    You're sure to be quietly overwhelmed, either by the number of stars or the way the moonlight reflects off of the granite domes surrounding the valley. See chapter 3.

**Tenaya Lake in Yosemite**    The solitude and beauty of this high-altitude crystal-clear lake outshine others in the park. Tenaya Lake is larger and dramatic, edging up against granite and reflecting boulders off its surface. See chapter 3.

**Hospital Rock in Sequoia**    Take the walk down the path near the rock, toward the water. Once there, explore eddies and pools created by the force of the river. You can actually climb around and through one intimidating boulder to a semihard-to-reach beach. See chapter 6.

# 2

# Planning Your Trip

*I*n the pages that follow, you'll find all the information you need before setting off on your adventure in one of these three breathtaking national parks.

## 1 Getting Started: Information & Reservations

For both parks, there are reams of visitor information available by phone, in bookstores, and on the Internet, but the National Park Service is the best place to start.

### FOR YOSEMITE

If you're planning a visit to Yosemite National Park, you can get general information on accommodations, weather, and permits from their Touch-Tone phone menu at ☎ 209/372-0200 or online at **www.nps.gov/yose/**. A live operator is available weekdays from 8am to 4:30pm at ☎ 900/454-YOSE. The hearing impaired can obtain information by calling ☎ 209/372-4726.

As this book went to press, the National Park Service had just selected a new company to handle their camping reservations for parks across the country. Biospherics, Inc., a Maryland-based company, is expected to be up and running by March 15, 1998. To make a reservation to camp in Yosemite National Park, call ☎ 800/436-7275. If you are unsuccessful using this number, try the general Yosemite information line at ☎ 209/372-0200.

Another great resource is YATI, or the Yosemite Area Travellers Information (☎ 209/723-3153, or online at www.yosemite.com). Also, the Yosemite Association is a nonprofit organization that publishes books and interpretive information for visitors (☎ 209/379-2646, or online at www.yosemite.org).

Information on lodging and activities outside the park is available from visitor centers and chambers of commerce in surrounding cities. If you're coming from the west on Highway 120, call the Tuolumne County Visitor Center at ☎ 800/446-1333. On Highway 140, call the Mariposa Town Center at ☎ 800/208-2434 or 209/966-2456. On Highway 41 south of the park, call the Yosemite Sierra Visitors Bureau at ☎ 209/683-4636. From Lee Vining on the park's eastern boundary, call the Lee Vining Chamber of Commerce at ☎ **619/647-6629** or 619/647-6595.

## FOR SEQUOIA/KINGS CANYON

Start with the National Park Service web site at **www.nps.gov/seki/** for the most up-to-date information on the park, lodging, hikes, regulations, and best times to visit. Much of the same information plus road conditions are available by phone (☎ **209/565-3341**). A live operator can be reached daily from 8am to 4:30pm (☎ **209/565-3134**).

For lodging information, call ☎ **209/335-5500.** Information on lodging and activities outside but near the park can be obtained from the Three Rivers Reservation Centre (☎ **209/561-0410,** or on the web at www.sequoiapark.com).

Camping reservations for Sequoia/Kings Canyon should be directed to Biospherics, Inc. at ☎ **800/365-2267.** Again, as we went to press, this service was not up and running, but was expected to be so as of March 15, 1998. If you are unsuccessful using this number, try the general Sequoia/Kings Canyon information line at ☎ **209/565-3341.**

## 2 When to Go

Both Yosemite and Sequoia/Kings Canyon are open year-round, but planning your visit in advance is always a good idea.

**YOSEMITE**   In this park, we recommend avoiding holiday weekends in spring and summer if possible—on 12 days in 1995 alone, the park had to turn people away from the valley due to overcrowding. The campgrounds (see chapter 5) are usually full from June through August, and expect some crowds in late spring and early fall as well. Winter is a great time to visit Yosemite—not only is the park virtually empty but there are a number of activities from skiing at Badger Pass to sledding, ice-skating, and snowshoeing. Keep in mind, however, that the high country along Highway 120 and Tioga Pass Road is inaccessible to vehicles from mid-fall to early June, depending on snow levels.

**SEQUOIA/KINGS CANYON**   Like Yosemite, there are a variety of attractions to these parks all year, but Cedar Grove is closed from mid-November to mid-April and Mineral King is closed from November 1 until Memorial Day weekend. Summertime supports a lively population of adventure seekers, including river rafters (see chapter 4), but hiking trail passes in the high country may be snowbound until July.

## CLIMATE

Yosemite and Sequoia/Kings Canyon, for the most part, share a climate that varies considerably depending on the region of the park. A good rule of thumb throughout the parks is to remember that the higher you go, the cooler it gets. So pack a parka on any trip that climbs above the valley floor or ventures into the backcountry.

During the summer, temperatures at lower elevations (such as Yosemite Valley) can climb into the 90s and higher, and plummet into the 50s at night. Afternoon temperatures average in the 60s and 70s in spring and fall, and again, evenings are usually cool. Afternoon showers are fairly common year-round. Winter days average in the 40s and 50s, and it seldom drops below zero, although much of the land above 5,500 feet is buried beneath several feet of snow.

The high country receives up to 20 feet of snow half the year and visitors should be experienced in winter travel. From November to March, it is wise to expect snow and carry tire chains. Remember, particularly wet winters lead to incredibly stunning and powerful spring waterfalls, especially in Yosemite.

## SPECIAL EVENTS
### IN YOSEMITE

**Jan–Mar:** The Wawona Winter Bed & Breakfast Package. This includes a stay at the historic Wawona Hotel, in-room continental breakfast, and champagne. There is a 2-night minimum stay and guests must arrive on Thursday. Costs ranges from $76 to $97 per person, plus tax, based on double occupancy. This package comes with free Friday ski lift tickets. A similar package is available over Valentine's Day.

**Jan–Feb:** Chefs' Holidays. Yosemite hosts nationally renowned chefs, who share their secrets with participants. Each session concludes with a banquet in The Ahwahnee Dining Room. Cost is $75 per person, including gratuity but excluding alcohol. Two, three- and five-day packages that include overnight accommodations at The Ahwahnee and admission to two banquets are available for $580 to $1,200 plus tax, based on double occupancy.

**February:** The Ahwahnee Romance Package. This is an expensive treat for visitors and includes a 3-night stay for couples. Cost is $799 plus tax, based on double occupancy, and includes an in-room candlelight dinner, breakfast in bed one morning, a picnic lunch, and other small touches, such as a rose at arrival, cordials, and champagne.

**October:** The Wawona Autumn Golf Package. Cost is $76 per person, plus tax, based on double occupancy. The rate, good Sunday through Thursday, includes 2 nights of lodging in a room with a shared bath, daily breakfast, and nine holes of golf a day.

**Nov–Dec:** Vintners' Holiday. California's finest winemakers hold tastings in The Ahwahnee Great Lounge. Each session concludes with a Vintners' Banquet. The four-course gala event held in The Ahwahnee Dining Room pairs four wines with a specially selected food. Cost is $80 per person, including gratuities and wine.

**December 22, 24 and 25:** The Bracebridge Dinner. The event transports diners to 17th-century England. Servers wear costumes and the dining room is filled with music and song course upon course of delectable dishes. This popular event requires reservations, which are secured by lottery. Applications are available December 1 to January 15 and are due February 15 for the following year. Cost is $200 per person.

**December 31:** New Year's Eve Dinner. On New Year's Eve, the tenor for the night is set by a swing band and dinner dance. The same reservations system applies here as with the Bracebridge Dinner. The cost is also $200.

### IN SEQUOIA/KINGS CANYON

The annual Christmas Tree Ceremony is the only event held here. It's always scheduled for the second Sunday in December and includes a solemn but moving tribute paid beneath the branches of the General Grant Tree, officially known as the Nation's Christmas Tree. The General Grant Tree is in Grant Grove.

## 3   Permits You Can Get in Advance

You'll need a permit to camp overnight in the backcountry of either park (see chapters 3, 4, 6, and 7). Permits are free, but it's a good idea to reserve one in advance during high season, and for that there's a fee of $3. For permits in Yosemite, call ☎ **209/372-0200** or stop by any Wilderness Permit Station or the Valley Wilderness Center. In Sequoia/Kings Canyon, call ☎ **209/565-3341.** Permits here are $10. Information is also available online at **www.nps.gov/ yose/** in Yosemite or **www.nps.gov/seki/** in Sequoia/Kings Canyon.

Yosemite loves to host weddings, but you'll need a permit for that, too. Information on wedding permits is available by phone at ☎ **209/379-1860.** The cost is $150, and the event is subject to approval and must be scheduled a year in advance. Entrance fees are not waived for the bride, groom, or guests.

Elsewhere in the parks, the usual permits and regulations apply—if you're planning on fishing, make sure you have a California fishing license. If you're planning on exploring the backcountry of either park, you'll need to apply for a wilderness permit. For more information on the process, refer to the "Exploring the Backcountry" sections of the appropriate "Exploring" chapters.

## 4 Getting There

### YOSEMITE
### BY PLANE

**Fresno Air Terminal** is the nearest major airport, located 90 miles from the South Entrance at Wawona (☎ **209/498-4095** from 8am to 8pm daily). It is served by American Air, American Eagle, Delta, Sky West United Airlines, United Express, US Airways, and Wings West. It has direct connections with airports in San Francisco and Los Angeles.

**Merced Airport** is 73 miles from the Arch Rock Entrance. It is served by United Express (☎ **800/241-6522**).

**Mariposa Airport** (☎ **209/966-2143**) has a tiny airstrip with space for 50 private planes.

### BY CAR

Yosemite is a 3$^1$/$_2$-hour drive from San Francisco and a 6-hour drive from Los Angeles. Many roads lead to Yosemite's four entrances. From the west, the Big Oak Flat Entrance is 88 miles from Manteca via Highway 120 and passes through the towns of Groveland, Buck Meadows, and Big Oak Flat. The Arch Rock Entrance is 75 miles northeast of Merced via Highway 140 and passes through Mariposa and El Portal. The South Entrance from Wawona is 64 miles north of Fresno and passes through Oakhurst, Bass Lake, and Fish Camp. From the east, the Tioga Pass Entrance is the only option. It is 10 miles west of Lee Vining via Highway 120.

### BY BUS

Daily bus transportation from Fresno, Merced, and Mariposa is provided by **VIA Bus Lines** (☎ **800/369-PARK**). Buses are not subject to park entrance delays during peak season. From Fresno, passengers pay $20 each way, with children 3 to 11 paying half price, and board at the airport at 2pm. From Merced, there are several departures daily from the airport and the Greyhound bus

# Highway Access to the Parks

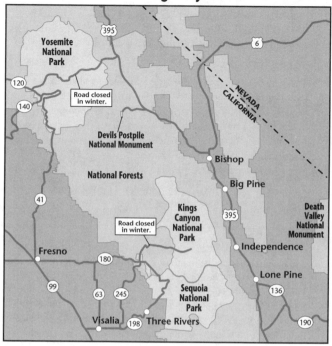

terminal. From Merced and Mariposa, reservations are necessary and should be made 24 hours in advance.

**Greyhound** (☎ **800/231-2222**) also links Fresno with many other California cities.

## BY TRAIN

**Amtrak** (☎ **800/872-7245**) also has routes to Fresno and Merced from many cities. In both cases, riders can connect to VIA Bus Lines to Yosemite.

## SEQUOIA/KINGS CANYON
## BY PLANE

Once again, **Fresno Air Terminal** (☎ **209/498-4095** from 8am to 8pm daily) is the nearest major airport, located 53 miles from the Big Stump Entrance in Kings Canyon. It is served by American Airlines, American Eagle, Delta, Sky West United Airlines, United Express, US Airways, and Wings West. It has direct connections with airports in San Francisco and Los Angeles.

**Visalia Municipal Airport** (☎ **209/738-3201**) is 36 miles from the Ash Mountain Entrance and is a tiny airstrip. The airport is served by United Express (☎ **800/241-6522**).

## BY CAR

There are two entrances to the parks—Highway 198 via Visalia and the town of Three Rivers leads to the Ash Mountain Entrance in Sequoia National Park, and Highway 180 via Fresno leads straight to the Big Stump Entrance near Grant Grove in Kings Canyon National Park. Both entrances are approximately 4 hours from Los Angeles and 5 hours from San Francisco.

## BY BUS

Greyhound and Trailways (☎ **800/231-2222**) serve Visalia and Fresno.

## RENTAL CARS

Although not available in either of the parks, most of the major car-rental companies can be found in Fresno: **Avis** (☎ **800/331-1212** or 209/454-5029); **National** (☎ **800/227-7368** or 209/251-5577); **Hertz** (☎ **800/654-3131** or 209/251-5055); **Standard** (☎ **800/ 953-2277** or 209/252-0555); **Budget** (☎ **800/527-0700** or 209/ 251-5515); **Sears** (☎ **800/527-0770** or 209/251-5517); and **Dollar** (☎ **800/800-4000** or 209/294-8001).

**RVs** are another option, although the parks reserve little space for these behemoths. There are several options for reservations. In Modesto, try **California RV Rentals** (☎ 209/523-2131). In Fresno, call **Cruise America Motor Home Rentals & Sales** (☎ 209/498-8445). When traveling by RV, however, it's important to call the park ahead of time and inquire about any vehicle length restrictions.

## 5  Learning Vacations & Special Programs

The **Yosemite Institute** (☎ **209/379-9511**) is one of the most reputable organizations within the park. This nonprofit organization offers a unique environment for learning about nature and the history of the Sierra Nevada. The institute caters mostly to grade-school students, but they're happy to accommodate groups of 12 or more in any age group. It also offers a host of weekend programs throughout the year. Participants can explore wildflowers in spring, or strap on snowshoes and explore how plants and animals adapt to the environment in winter. Special family camps are offered during the holidays.

**Incredible Adventures** (☎ 800/777-8464) offers 3-day trips and hikes to Yosemite from San Francisco. The trip is a flat fee that varies depending on the excursion and includes all food and transportation. The guide-to-traveler ratio is 1:14.

**Outward Bound** (☎ 888/882-6863) is a reputable school founded on the belief that respect for self and others leads to a respect of the environment. The organization provides 1- and 2-week courses in the Sierra region that includes Yosemite. Activities and dates vary.

**Yosemite Field Seminars** (☎ 209/379-2321) offers 70 outdoor field seminars each year. Courses are taught in natural history, photography, day hikes, backpacking trips, California Native American Studies, writing, painting, poetry, and more. Topics range from "Words in the Wild: A Writing Retreat" to "Mammals of the High Sierra." Costs range from $45 to $265 and include all park fees and a shared campsite or room. Class size ranges from 6 to 20 people.

**Sequoia Natural History Association** (☎ 209/565-3728) offers a number of field seminars in and around Sequoia and Kings Canyon national parks. Topics range from hiking, mountaineering, and spelunking to photography, stargazing, and botanizing. Call for their brochure or visit them on the web at http://home.inreach.com/a-seqnha.

## 6  Tips for Travelers with Disabilities

People visit these parks to witness their beauty, and that can be done in a host of different ways—you don't have to hike 5 miles or climb a waterfall. Some of the most rewarding moments come from quiet observation.

*Tip:* Be sure to inquire about the free Golden Access Pass available to the blind and permanently disabled in either park. Information is available at the entrances and visitor centers.

Yosemite is fair when it comes to accommodating those with disabilities. Restaurants and some of the rooms at the lodge and the Ahwahnee are wheelchair accessible. There are some paved trails around the valley floor, including ones to Mirror Lake and Happy Isles, that are fairly level. Ask for information on accessible points when making reservations.

In Sequoia/Kings Canyon, the visitor centers in the Foothills, Lodgepole, and Grant Grove are wheelchair accessible. Paved trails lead to the General Sherman Tree and General Grant Tree. In Giant Forest, there are a few paved trails (including the aptly named

Trail for all People). There are modified picnic tables at Hospital Rock and Big Stump. Special requests should be directed to ☎ 209/ 565-3134.

## 7 Tips for Travelers with Pets

Few national parks make traveling with pets fun. But, if you choose to, be prepared for stern limitations. There are no pets allowed on unpaved trails, they must be on a leash at all times, and may never be left alone. Pets must stay on paved paths in the valley and elsewhere. Pets are not permitted in any lodging facility, store, or restaurant in the park. The places that do allow your four-legged friends in Yosemite are the Upper Pines Campground in the valley, Crane Flat, Hodgdon Meadow, White Wolf, Yosemite Creek, and Tuolumne Meadows campgrounds.

Sequoia/Kings Canyon has similar regulations. Pets are allowed in all campgrounds but not on any trails or in the backcountry. A good rule of thumb issued by the Park Service: You can take your pet wherever you can take your car, but keep him on a leash.

## 8 Tips for Travelers with Children

Bringing huge things down to a kid's level is half the battle in helping youngsters enjoy the wilderness. The other half is allowing enough time for spontaneous exploration and fun. We're not suggesting an impromptu rafting trip down the Kings River, but easy games, such as naming the animals that rely on the river, tend to while away the in-between time.

Yosemite offers a number of kids' programs that make adults envious. Since everything in the park is huge beyond comprehension, they have planned activities that attempt to bring the park down to kids' size. Children age 8 to 12 can sign up for the Junior and Senior Rangers program, which hooks them up with a national park ranger who helps the children discover nature and the secret places in the valley. Kids receive a patch after completion. Registration is at the Happy Isles Nature Center (shuttle bus stop No. 16) and the program is offered June through August.

Ranger-led walks begin at the Yosemite Valley Visitor Center (shuttle bus stop Nos. 6 and 9). These vary by season. Check the visitor center for information. Free nature walks and talks are available daily at no cost. Check your Yosemite Guide (handed out at park entrances) for departure times and topics. The Indian Cultural

Museum (shuttle bus stop Nos. 6 and 9) has exhibits and brief lectures conducted by descendants of Yosemite's first residents. The Happy Isles Nature Center (shuttle bus stop No. 16) has displays and dioramas of park animals that children will enjoy.

Unlike in Yosemite, there are very few kids-only events in Sequoia/Kings Canyon. One option is the Walter Fry Nature Center located in the Lodgepole Campground, open during summer only. Other than that, check bulletin boards or visitor centers for locally scheduled activities, or you might try some of the shorter hikes with frequent rewards—waterfalls, wildflowers, historic buildings—to keep youngsters interested. It might also help to bone up on your natural history beforehand. Grab a children's book that tells the difference between a sugar and ponderosa pine, or explains in understandable terms how much a Giant Sequoia weighs.

## 9  Protecting Your Health & Safety

Common sense and personal responsibility are always your best guide in national parks, but here are some of the basics.

- While some of the bridges that cross rivers and streams look inviting, resist the temptation to use them as a diving board.
- Trails, especially ones over rock and granite, can be slick. Be especially careful along any rivers or creeks, such as Mist Trail in Yosemite, where wind and water can make for treacherous conditions. Drowning is the most common cause of accidental death throughout the national parks.
- Always carry more than enough water—sometimes 1- and 2-mile walks can easily turn into 5- and 6-mile hikes.
- Under no circumstances should food be left in tents, cabins, or cars. The bear population is healthy in these parks (especially Sequoia/Kings Canyon) and in some cases fearless. There are storage lockers and bear-proof containers throughout the park—use them.
- Under no circumstances should you feed a bear, or any animal for that matter. Sure it's a thrill, but if the prospect of being bitten by a squirrel doesn't send shivers up your spine try this: When animals become dependent on human food, they quit foraging and begin harassing travelers for meals. Most often, this results in the animal's demise as park rangers take a dim view of troublesome pests, which are quickly put down.
- Always carry a map if you go hiking, even for short day hikes.

## 10   Protecting the Environment

Don't feed the animals. Don't litter. Don't take anything home you didn't buy or bring with you. Share trails and walkways, and stay on them. If this sounds like something you learned in grade school, it is, but you'll be surprised by the antics you'll witness in Yosemite. People think nothing of packing home a few extra rocks, pine cones, and saplings. Cigarette butts are regularly stubbed out on trails, food wrappers frequently land on the ground near trash cans, and initials are engraved in wood. Sometimes, people need a gentle reminder that 50 million years of work deserves a little respect, especially if they want to revisit the park in years to come.

Amid the litany of environmental troubles already discussed, air pollution is a particular threat to these parks. Therefore, whenever possible, avoid starting your car. Try to consolidate trips or walk when covering a short distance. If everyone pitches in, the effects of pollution will be decreased.

# 3

# Exploring Yosemite

*Y*osemite's skyscraping geologic formations, lush meadows, swollen rivers, and spectacular waterfalls make it a tourist destination for travelers from around the world. It's home to three of the world's 10 tallest waterfalls and the largest single piece of exposed granite anywhere. It has one of the world's largest trees and the most recognized rock formation. The greatest thing about all this is you don't have to be a mountaineer to enjoy the beauty. Yosemite's most popular attractions are accessible to everyone, whether they want to hike around or just stand and stare. No matter where you go, you'll see a view worth remembering.

## 1 Essentials

### ACCESS/ENTRY POINTS

There are four entrances to Yosemite: the Big Oak Flat Entrance and the Arch Rock Entrance from the west, the South Entrance, and the Tioga Pass Entrance in the northeast. Refer to the map on page 23 ("Highway Access to the Parks") for exact locations of entry points.

### VISITOR CENTERS & INFORMATION

In the park, the best and biggest visitor center is the Valley Visitor Center in Yosemite Village (☎ 209/372-0299). The center offers tour information, daily ranger programs, lodging, and restaurants. The rangers who staff the center are helpful, insightful, and knowledgeable. Inside, information boards update road conditions and campsite availability, and serve as a message board. Maps, books, and videos can also be purchased. There are several exhibits on the park, its geologic history, and the history of the valley. This center also has information on bears as well as the human impact on the park. Nearby is Yosemite Valley Wilderness Center, a small room with high country maps, information on necessary equipment, and trail information. A ranger at the desk can answer all your questions, issue permits, and offer advice about the high country. Elsewhere, the Wawona Information Station (☎ 209/375-9501) and Big Oak Flat Information Center (☎ 209/379-1899) give general park information. In the high country, the Tuolumne Meadows Visitor

Center (☎ **209/372-0263**) is helpful. Questions about visitor-related services, including accommodations, can be accessed at ☎ **209/372-1000**.

## FEES

It costs $20 per car per week to enter the valley, or $10 per person per week if arriving on bicycle or on foot.

It costs $3 to $15 a night to camp in a Yosemite campground (☎ **800/436-7275**). Prices are subject to change without notice. Book months in advance to stay during the summer. But it's worth checking back because cancellations do occur. Reservations are accepted in 1-month blocks beginning on the 15th of each month. Reservations can be made up to 3 months in advance. That said, make your reservations as near to the 15th of the month 3 months in advance of when you want to stay in the park, especially for sites in the valley. Additional campground information is available by Touch-Tone phone (☎ **209/372-0200**).

## REGULATIONS

In Yosemite National Park, there is a 7-day camping limit in the valley and Wawona, and a 14-day limit elsewhere from May 1 to September 15. For the remaining months of the year, there is a 30-day limit. Some campgrounds inside and outside the valley are closed in winter. Some outside the valley are first-come, first-served. A maximum of six people and two vehicles may stay at each campsite. Checkout is at noon. Pets are allowed in a few campgrounds.

## SPECIAL DISCOUNTS & PASSES

The Yosemite Pass is a bargain at $40 for a year. The National Park Service also sells the Golden Eagle Pass, which costs $50 for a year and provides entrance to all national parks. Senior citizens (62 and older) can purchase a lifetime Golden Age Pass for $10. The blind and permanently disabled are eligible for the free Golden Access Pass. Passes are available at the gates, or a ranger will provide directions to park purchase stations. The Golden Access Pass is only available at the Yosemite Valley Visitor Center.

### FAST FACTS: Yosemite National Park

**ATMs**   A machine can be found in a hub of buildings next to the Yosemite Village Store.

**Car Trouble/Towing Services**   Call ☎ **911** for all emergencies, but for car trouble in the park, call ☎ 372-1001.

**Climate**    See chapter 2.

**Emergencies**    Call ☎ **911.**

**Gas Stations**    There are two gas stations in Yosemite, in the town of Wawona and at Crane Flat, just outside the valley.

**Laundromats**    Yosemite has Laundromats at Housekeeping Camp and Yosemite Lodge, both in the valley.

**Maps**    The best maps of Yosemite are published by the Yosemite Association and sell for $2.50 at just about every location in the park. Each map (they're green and white, and fold out accordion style) covers a specific region—the valley, Wawona, Tuolumne—and includes all pertinent information such as parking, hiking trails, elevations, accommodations, ranger stations, the natural history of each region, and rest rooms. In general, these won't do if you're planning a lengthy hike, but they will work for general directions and to help with the lay of the land. They add vital detail to the overall park map handed free to visitors at all entrances.

**Medical/Dental Clinics**    Yosemite has a medical and dental clinic. Both are in the valley, near Yosemite Village. The Yosemite Medical Clinic can be reached at ☎ **209/372-4637.** The dental clinic is at ☎ **209/372-4200.**

**Outfitters**    Those with regularly scheduled programs serve only Yosemite. Try the Yosemite Institute (☎ **209/379-9511**), a nonprofit organization offering a unique environment for learning about nature and the human history of the Sierra Nevada. Also check Incredible Adventures (☎ **800/777-8464**), which offers 3-day trips and hikes to Yosemite from San Francisco. Yosemite Field Seminars (☎ **209/379-2321**) offers 70 outdoor field seminars each year. Yosemite Creek Outfitters leads fly-fishing trips in Yosemite (☎ **209/962-5060**).

**Permits**    Required for all overnight camping in the backcountry (see chapter 4). Call ☎ **209/372-0200** in Yosemite, or stop by any Wilderness Permit Station or the Valley Wilderness Center.

**Post Offices**    In Yosemite, there are post offices in Yosemite Village and Wawona. During the summer, a mail drop is also located at the general store in Tuolumne Meadows.

**Supplies**    The best selection in Yosemite is at the Village Store. Also check markets in Curry Village and Yosemite Lodge. Markets can also be found in Wawona and Tuolumne Meadows.

**Weather**    Updates for Yosemite are available by Touch-Tone phone at ☎ **209/372-0200,** or online at **www.nps.gov/yose/**.

## 2  Orientation

All four main entrances to the park meet in Yosemite Valley, the most popular of the park's three destination points (the other two being Tuolumne Meadows and Wawona). The valley is a mile wide and 7 miles long, set at about 4,000 feet above sea level. The granite walls of Half Dome, El Capitan, and Glacier Point (see chapter 4) tower another 4,000 feet overhead. The picturesque Merced River, fed by several small brooks and creeks, winds lazily through the length of Yosemite Valley. In January of 1997, the creek and river, swollen after a heavy winter, washed across the valley floor, submerging almost everything beneath 2 feet of water. Some damage still remains.

It's relatively easy to find your way around Yosemite. All road signs are clear and visible. Although at first Yosemite Valley may appear a confusing series of roadways, you'll soon realize that everything leads to a one-way road that hugs the valley's perimeter. To get from one side to the other, you can either drive the entire loop or travel one of the few bridges over the Merced River. It is, however, easy to find yourself heading in the wrong direction on the one-way road, so be alert whenever you merge and just follow the signs.

In addition to the year-round shuttle bus in Yosemite Valley, Wawona and Tuolumne Meadows offer a similar service during summer months only. Driving in any of these places during peak season—or even off-season in the valley—is a surefire way to ensure that you'll miss important sights, get stuck in traffic, and hate your vacation. Summer months are particularly bad and you'd have to be nuts to want to try and navigate around all the crazy tourists (of course not you), cyclists, and other road warriors, so be bright and park the car whenever possible.

A second benefit to parking is that almost as soon as you're out of eyesight of your vehicle, you have ceased to become a typical Yosemite tourist. Most park visitors never get more than a couple of miles from their car.

### YOSEMITE VALLEY

Face it, most people come to Yosemite to see this giant study in shadow and light. In spring, after winter snow begins melting in the High Country, waterfalls encircle Yosemite Valley, shimmering like a diamond necklace. Careful observers can watch rock climbers inch up the massive granite face of El Capitan or Half Dome. There are wide, beautiful meadows, towering trees, and the ever-present sound of rushing water in the background. The great irony is that the original park boundaries, established in 1890, excluded the valley. In addition to the natural phenomena throughout the valley, there are a number of historical attractions worth exploring as well.

Yosemite Valley consists of three developed areas. All the hotels, restaurants, and shops can be found in **Yosemite Village, Yosemite Lodge,** and **Curry Village,** and all campgrounds are within walking distance of these places. Curry Village (also called Camp Curry) and Yosemite Lodge offer the bulk of the park's overnight accommodations. Curry Village is near shuttle bus stop Nos. 1, 13, and 14. Yosemite Lodge is served by stop No. 8. Both locations have restaurants and a small grocery. The lodge has a large public swimming pool, and Curry Village has an ice rink open in winter.

**Yosemite Village** is the largest developed region within the valley and is served by shuttle bus stop Nos. 3, 5, 6, 9, and 10. It is home to the park's largest visitor center and headquarters for the National Park Service in Yosemite, as well as Yosemite Concession Services, which has the contract to run all park accommodations and restaurants. The village also has a host of stores and shops, including a grocery, restaurants, and the valley's only medical clinic, dentist, post office, beauty shop, and ATM.

Also, check out the **Yosemite Pioneer Cemetery,** a peaceful graveyard in the shade of tall sequoias with headstones dating back to the 1800s. Funny, but nothing about this place is morbid. There are about 36 marked graves, identifiable by horizontal slabs of rock, some etched with crude or faded writing. There are some notables in Yosemite history buried here, such as James Lamon, an early settler, known for his apple trees that still bear fruit, who died in 1875. And there's the touching grave of 14-year-old Effie Maud Crippen, who died August 31, 1881, after "she faltered by the wayside and the angels took her home."

Next door, you'll find the **Yosemite Museum and Indian Cultural Exhibit.** Both are free and provide a historic picture of the park, before and after it was settled and secured as a national treasure. The museum entrance is marked by a crowd-pleaser, the cross-section of a 1,000-year-old sequoia with memorable dates identified on the tree's rings. Highlights include the signing of the Magna Carta in 1215, the landing of Columbus in the New World, and the Civil War. The ring was cut in 1919 from a tree that fell in the Mariposa Grove south of the valley in Wawona. The Indian Cultural Exhibit strives to explain the life of Native Americans who once lived here, and Native Americans regularly speak or give demonstrations

# Yosemite Valley

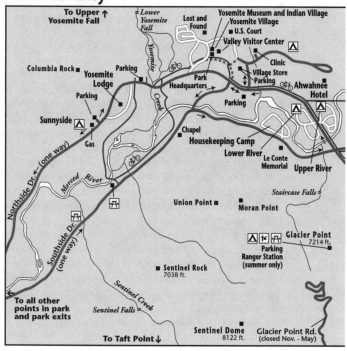

in long-forgotten arts such as basket weaving. Kids seem to get a real kick out of this.

The village of **Ahwahnee** is behind the museum and Indian Cultural Exhibit. The village offers a free self-guided walking tour accessible from the back door of the visitor center. This exhibit accepts visitors through the transformation of the Ahwahneeche, the tribe that inhabited Yosemite Valley until the mid-1850s. The village includes a ceremonial roundhouse that's still in use.

The **Ansel Adams Gallery** is open daily from 9am to 6pm. Prints and cards of photographs made famous by Adams are available for purchase. The shop also serves as a small gallery for current artisans, some with works for sale.

East of Yosemite Village on a narrow, dead-end road is the majestic old **Ahwahnee Hotel** (see chapter 5). Take the shuttle bus to stop No. 4. It's definitely worth a visit for anyone interested in architecture and design.

There's a small chapel on the south side of the Merced River, shuttle bus stop No. 11. The chapel holds worship services posted

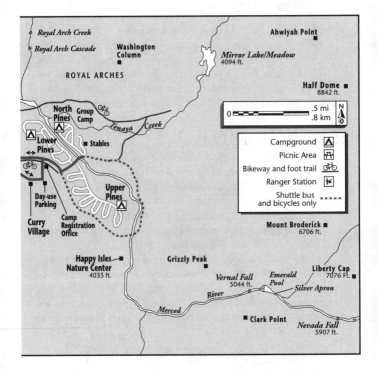

in the Yosemite Guide and available by phone (☎ 209/372-4831). From the bus stop, walk across the bridge and to the left for just under a quarter-mile.

The **LeConte Memorial Lodge** is an educational center and library at shuttle bus stop No. 12. Built in 1903 in honor of a University of California geologist named Joseph LeConte, the Tudor-style granite building provides discussions free of charge. Talks are listed in the Yosemite Guide.

At the valley's far east end beyond Curry Village is the **Happy Isles Nature Center,** shuttle bus stop No. 16. The center is closed in the winter. Summer hours are 9am to 5pm daily, with spring and fall hours as posted. This new structure was built after a deadly rock slide damaged the previous quarters. A huge slab of granite high up on a wall behind the building crashed to earth in late 1996 with such force that it created a 120-m.p.h. gust of wind that flattened about 500 trees. Although some of the trees are gone, the remnants of the rock slide remain. Happy Isles is named for three nearby inlets labeled by Yosemite's guardian in 1880. Happy Isles itself serves as the

trailhead for some great hikes listed in chapter 4. The nature center offers exhibits and books on the various animal and plant life
found in Yosemite. There are exhibits on park animals, a night dis-
play, and more. It's a super place for children to explore, and we
know a couple of 30-something kids who had a great time here, too.
This is also the location of the park's Junior and Senior Ranger programs described later in this chapter.

## NORTH OF THE VALLEY

**Hetch Hetchy** and **Tuolumne Meadows** are remarkably different
regions on opposite sides of the park. Hetch Hetchy is on the park's
western border and can be reached by taking the turnoff just outside the park's Big Oak Flat Entrance. Tuolumne Meadows is on the
park's eastern border, just inside Tioga Pass. Both places are inaccessible by motor vehicle in the winter. In summer, Hetch Hetchy
gets hot and Tuolumne Meadows gets crowded.

Hetch Hetchy is home to the park's reviled reservoir, one fought
over for years by the famed conservationist John Muir. In the end,
Muir lost and the dam was built, ensuring water for the city of San
Francisco. Many believe the loss exhausted Muir and hastened his
death in 1914, a year after a bill was signed to fund the dam project.
Construction began in 1919.

South of Hetch Hetchy, inside the park, are two large stands of
Giant Sequoias. The Merced and Tuolumne Groves offer a quiet
alternative to the Mariposa Grove of Big Trees in Wawona. Both
groves are accessible only on foot. The Merced Grove is a 4-mile
round-trip walk that begins on Highway 120 about 4$^1/_2$ miles beyond the Big Oak Flat Entrance. While the trees don't mirror the
majesty of the Mariposa Grove, the solitude here makes this a real
treat for hikers. The Tuolumne Grove of about 25 trees can be
reached by a 1-mile hike (2 hrs. round-trip).

About 1$^1/_2$ hours east along Highway 120 is Yosemite's high
country. This primitive region is low on amenities, which makes it
a frequent haunt of those who enjoy roughing it—but even cushy-
soft couch potatoes can enjoy the beauty up here. Glistening granite domes tower above lush green meadows, cut by silver swaths of
streams and lakes. Many of Yosemite's longer hikes begin or pass
through here. The high country is explored at length in chapter 4,
but there are some worthwhile sights for anyone willing to venture
away from the valley masses.

**Olmsted Point,** located midway between White Wolf and
Tuolumne Meadows, offers one of the hands-down most spectacular

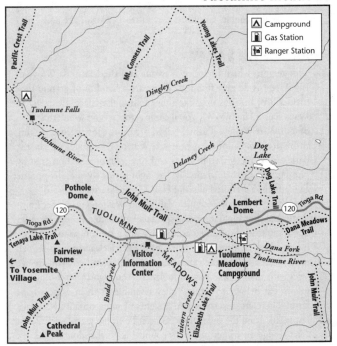

vistas anywhere in the park. Here the enormous walls of the Tenaya Canyon are exposed and an endless view stretches all the way to Yosemite Valley. In the distance are Cloud's Rest and the rear of Half Dome. To the east, Tenaya Lake glistens like a sapphire. One of the park's larger lakes, Tenaya is easily accessible, but the water is freezing.

About 8 miles east of Tenaya Lake is **Tuolumne Meadows,** a huge high country flat surrounded by domes and steep granite mountains that themselves offer exhilarating climbs. The meadow is a beautiful place to hike and fish, or just stand and gape. To the north of the meadow is Lembert Dome at about two o'clock, and then working clockwise, Johnson Peak at seven o'clock, Unicorn Peak, Fairview Dome at ten o'clock, and Pothole Dome. Up the road is the central region of Tuolumne, a crowded conglomerate of buildings that includes a visitor center, campground, canvas tent-cabins, and grocery. The real draw here is the scenery and lack of valley crowds. But in July and August, the small confines make it just as intolerable. Continue east to reach Tioga Lake and Tioga Pass.

## SOUTH OF THE VALLEY

This region, which includes Wawona and the Mariposa Grove of Big Trees, is densely forested. There are a handful of granite rock formations, but nothing like those found elsewhere. En route to Wawona on Highway 41, you'll come across several wonderful views of Yosemite Valley. Tunnel View, a turnout just before passing through a long tunnel en route to Wawona, provides one of the park's most recognizable vistas and one memorialized on film by photographer Ansel Adams. To the right is Bridalveil Fall, opposite El Capitan. Yosemite Falls and Half Dome lie straight ahead.

Halfway between Yosemite Valley and Wawona is Glacier Point Road, the thoroughfare to the spectacular **Glacier Point,** 16 miles down the road. From the parking area, it's a short hike to an amazing overlook that provides a view of the glacier-carved granite rock formations all along the valley and beyond. From here, you are eye level with Half Dome, which looks close enough to reach out and touch. Far below, Yosemite Valley resembles a green-carpeted ant farm. There are also some pretty sights of more obscure waterfalls not visible from the valley floor. Glacier Point has a geology hut and a new lodge for wintertime cross-country skiers that doubles the rest of the year as a gift store/snack shack. It's accessible by bus and foot (both methods are described later in this chapter).

Continue south on Highway 41 to reach **Wawona,** a small town 30 miles from the valley that runs deep with history. It was settled in 1856 by homesteader Galen Clark, who built a rustic waystation for travelers en route from Mariposa to Yosemite. The property's next owners, the Washburn brothers, built much of what is today the Wawona Hotel, including the large white building to the right of the main hotel, which was constructed in 1876. The two-story hotel annex went up 3 years later. When Congress established Yosemite National Park in 1890 and charged the U.S. Army with managing it, Wawona was chosen as the Army's headquarters. Every summer, soldiers would camp in what today is the Wawona Campground. For 16 summers, the cavalry out of San Francisco occupied the camp and mapped the park. When Yosemite Valley was added after the turn of the century, the cavalry picked up and relocated to the valley.

As Yosemite grew in popularity, so did the Wawona Hotel and the town itself. When the Wawona Hotel was added to the park in

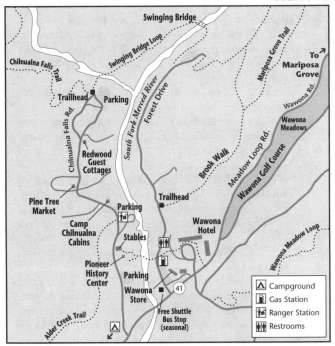

1932, Section 35 (the number assigned to the plot in its legal description) was allowed to remain in private ownership. It remains today, just east of the hotel off of Highway 41. Unless you're hiking or staying here in a private home or cabin, there is no real reason to venture along the narrow road that leads to the town. In fact, the number and collection of buildings can be depressing.

The public Wawona is much more enjoyable. The Mariposa Grove is a stand of Giant Sequoias, some of which have been around for 3,000 years. They stretch almost 300 feet tall, are 50 feet in circumference, and weigh an average of 2 million pounds. The 500 trees here are divided into the Upper Grove and Lower Grove. The easiest way to see the trees is on an open-air tram that runs during summer. At the time of this printing, the cost is $8 for adults, $7.25 for seniors, $4 for children. Kids under age 4 are free. A family pass costs $24 and admits 2 adults and all the kids in the crew between the ages of 4 and 15. Trams leave every 20 minutes. The trip is narrated by a guide and lasts about an hour. It makes regular stops at the Grizzly Giant, Wawona Tunnel Tree, and Mariposa Grove Museum. It's worth hopping out and walking around as often as possible. Just take the next tram back. All of this is also accessible on foot. It is an uphill walk to the upper grove, 2.5 miles each way.

The Grizzly Giant is the largest tree in the grove. At "just" 200 feet it is shorter than some of its neighbors, but its trunk measures more than 30 feet in diameter at the base. A huge limb halfway up measures 6 feet in diameter and is bigger than many of the "young" trees in the grove. Some say that limb is larger than any tree east of the Mississippi.

The Wawona Tunnel Tree had a tunnel 10 feet high and 26 feet long cut through it in 1881. Thousands of visitors were photographed driving through the tree before it toppled in the winter of 1968–69—its death was caused by heavy snow. (The tree had been weakened by the tunnel and its shallow root system.) No one saw the tree fall. Another tunnel tree, the California Tree, cut in 1895, still stands near the Grizzly Giant.

The Mariposa Grove Museum was the first building built by Galen Clark. It was last refurbished in 1981, and during the summer there are exhibits, and books and educational materials are sold.

Near the Wawona Hotel are the Thomas Hill Studio and Pioneer Yosemite History Center. The studio, which keeps sporadic hours that are impossible to pin down but are frequently listed in the Yosemite Guide, is the former workspace of noted 19th-century painter Thomas Hill. He came to Wawona in 1885 after his daughter married a Washburn. Hill painted a number of award-winning landscapes, including some recognizable ones of Yosemite.

The Pioneer Center offers a self-guided walking tour of cabins and buildings moved to this site in 1961 from various locations in the park. Each represents a different time in Yosemite's short history. During the summer, the National Park Service interpreters dress in period clothing and act out characters from the park's past. To reach the Pioneer Center, walk across the covered bridge. An entertaining 10-minute stagecoach ride is offered from here for a small fee.

## 3  The Highlights

**Yosemite Falls** is a two-part waterfall that stretches 2,700 feet skyward, making it one of the tallest waterfalls in the world. In spring, runoff makes this a magnificent spectacle as spray crashes to the base and leaves visitors drenched. In winter, cold temperatures help form

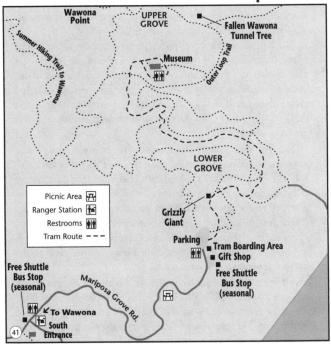

Wawona
Point

UPPER
GROVE

Fallen Wawona
Tunnel Tree

Summer Hiking Trail to Wawona

Outer Loop Trail

Museum

LOWER
GROVE

**Picnic Area** 🏕
**Ranger Station** 🏠
**Restrooms** 🚻
**Tram Route** - - -

Grizzly
Giant

Parking

Tram Boarding Area
Gift Shop
Free Shuttle
Bus Stop
(seasonal)

Free Shuttle
Bus Stop
(seasonal)

Mariposa Grove Rd.

To Wawona
South
Entrance

41

a cone at the base of the waterfall, sometimes reaching 300 feet high, like a giant upside-down snowcone. You can reach the base of Yosemite Falls by taking the shuttle bus to stop No. 7. It is also an easy walk from any parking lot near Yosemite Lodge.

**Mirror Lake** is a picturesque puddle located just out of the mid-valley fray. Named for the nearly perfect way it reflects the surrounding scenery, the lake is slowly filling with sediments, and depending on spring runoff, may be little more than a watering hole by midsummer. Still, the lake captures beautiful images of Half Dome and North Dome, which tower above. It is surrounded by forest and has a fairly level paved trail along its banks, which also offer places to sunbathe and picnic. It's accessible to people with disabilities. Take the shuttle to stop No. 17.

The **Mist Trail** to Vernal Fall shows the power behind the water that flows through Yosemite. The trail itself can be slick and treacherous, but it is a pretty walk up 500 steps to the top of the waterfall (see chapter 4). Miniature rainbows dot the trail as mist from the waterfalls splashes below and ricochets back onto the trail. This walk is frequently closed in winter due to snow.

The remnants of a recent rock slide remain behind the Happy Isles Nature Center. This pile of rubble is a reminder of the geologic catastrophes that shaped this park. Several years ago, a granite slab collapsed with such force that it blew over hundreds of trees and claimed one life. The slide filled the valley with dust. Afterward, a decision was made to leave the landscape pretty much as it was after the slide.

The **view from Glacier Point** is one of the most spectacular vistas anywhere in the park. From the point far above the valley floor visitors will find themselves eye level with Half Dome and hundreds of feet above most waterfalls. The white and silver rocks offer stark contrast against the sky. To reach Glacier Point, take one of the buses (check at tour desks for information) or drive south of the valley on Highway 41 to the turnoff for Glacier Point Road. Follow the winding road to the parking lot and walk a few hundred yards to the lookout. This is an excellent spot for pictures.

A **drive toward the high country on Highway 120,** also known as Tioga Road and Tioga Pass Road, offers other breathtaking views, especially at Olmsted Point. The point is a great view of granite landscaping. There are nearby picnic spots at the picturesque Tenaya Lake. Further on is the emerald-green Tuolumne Meadows, which is dotted during late spring and summer with thousands of wildflowers (see "Exploring the Backcountry" in chapter 4).

An **off-season visit,** especially in winter, offers unique beauty plus the peace and quiet that must have once been commonplace in Yosemite. Snow dusts the granite peaks and valley floor, bends trees, and creates a wonderland for visitors. Lodging rates drop, and it is slightly easier to secure accommodations, but even a day trip can be very rewarding. Even though many animals hibernate during the cold months, this is the best time of year to see the valley as it was before it became such a popular place.

## 4 How to See the Park in 1 or 2 Days

If you're like most visitors to Yosemite, you'll stick to the valley and stay less than 2 nights. It's ironic, considering the immensity and grandeur of the property, but if you have limited time, don't despair—there's a lot to see and do. Following are some attractions that will give you the most Yosemite flavor in just a little time.

Most importantly, learn two very important words—*shuttle bus.* Dump your car and pick up a bus schedule—it will quickly become your friend. *Note:* If you don't plan to stay overnight, use the Curry Village day-use parking lot to catch the shuttle. The bus is free, easy to use, and operates year-round, with fewer stops in winter. For that reason, we've included shuttle bus stop numbers wherever possible throughout the valley sections in this book. Bus stops are well marked and within easy walking distance from all parking lots.

The Valley Visitor Center (shuttle bus stop Nos. 6 and 9) is your logical starting point. Here, you'll see and hear an orientation on how the valley was created, learn about Yosemite's unique granite landscaping, and gain an appreciation and understanding of the park. More importantly, you can see what there is to see, orient yourself, and get back outside.

If you're not apt to take off on your own, one of the best ideas to spend your time wisely is taking one of the guided tours (see "Organized Tours & Ranger Programs," below). But if group activities aren't really your bag, try the following sites on your own:

The base of Lower Yosemite Fall (shuttle bus stop No. 7) is an easy walk from the parking lot across from Yosemite Lodge. The hike is described in greater detail in chapter 4. From here, you will be able to see a portion of the magnificent water show. During peak runoff, it's not uncommon to get wet as the force of the fall sends spray in every direction. In winter, a huge snowcone caused by freezing water rises to heights of up to 300 feet at the base of this fall.

Happy Isles (shuttle bus stop No. 16) is another major attraction. Located at the convergence of several inlets, it's the site of the valley's new nature center. This is also the trailhead for Vernal and Nevada falls, two picturesque staircase waterfalls that can be reached on foot. Both are described in chapter 4.

Next, we recommend a visit to Mirror Lake (shuttle bus stop No. 17), a small lake named for the near-perfect way it reflects the surrounding scenery. It's slowly filling up with silt and is less dramatic and mirrorlike than it used to be, but its shore still offers a beautiful view of Half Dome. This short stroll is well marked and described at length later on.

From there, if you have more time, there's a variety of hikes and activities at your disposal. Make the most of your time, and choose from our recommendations listed throughout the following chapters.

## 5   Driving in the Park

In the valley, it's like we said—*shuttle bus*. There are only two reasons to drive in Yosemite Valley: to enter or exit. And, as previously stated, there's a plan in action that may completely phase out day-use vehicles in the valley altogether over the next decade.

Elsewhere in the park, however, a vehicle is more appropriate. If you want to explore Wawona or Tuolumne, hike near Tenaya Lake, or check out Mariposa Grove, having your car is convenient, as at this time there is no direct bus service from the valley to Wawona/Mariposa Grove. Some sample package tours are described below, or inquire at tour desks in Yosemite Village, the Ahwahnee, Yosemite Lodge, and Curry Village, but the limited schedule and cost can be prohibitive. So until the Park Service decides whether to ban all private vehicles in the valley and institute a top-rate transportation system that reaches beyond the valley walls, automobile travel will remain necessary.

## 6   Organized Tours & Ranger Programs

Several organizations host tours to the valley from surrounding cities. Most go out of their way to accommodate guests, who benefit from not having to drive, skirting traffic jams and learning from experienced tour guides along the way.

**Bass Lake–Yosemite Tours** (☎ **209/877-8687**) conducts scheduled as well as customized trips. Costs range from $34 to $48, depending on the tour. Tours are operated on small air-conditioned buses with huge picture windows. The sightseeing includes Mariposa Grove, Yosemite Valley, and Glacier Point. Geology, flora, and fauna are pointed out along the way. Stops are scheduled for lunch, shopping, and photo opportunities. Pickup can be arranged from various motels throughout Oakhurst and Bass Lake.

If you're staying in the valley, the Park Service and Yosemite Concession Services present nearly a dozen evening programs that explore all aspects of the park's history and culture. In past summers, programs have included a discussion on early expeditions to Yosemite, the park's flora and fauna, and legends of Native Americans who once lived here. Other programs have focused on Mark Wellman's courageous climb of El Capitan—he made the ascent as a paraplegic—and the global ecology and major threats to Yosemite's environment.

Inquire about current programs upon check-in at your hotel or at the information booth outside the visitor center. While most programs are held in the valley, all major campgrounds in the park offer campfire programs throughout the week.

A number of guided walks are available. Check at one of the visitor centers or in the Yosemite Guide for current topics, start times, and locations. Walks may vary from week to week, but you can always count on nature hikes, evening discussions on park anomalies (floods, fires, or critters), and the sunrise photography program aimed at replicating some of Ansel Adams's works. Most do not require advanced registration—just show up at the appointed time and place. The sunrise photo walk always gets rave reviews from the early risers who venture out at dawn. The living history evening program outside at Yosemite Lodge is great for young and old alike.

A host of **guided bus tours** is also available. You can buy tickets at tour desks at Yosemite Lodge, the Ahwahnee, Curry Village, or beside the Village Store in Yosemite Village. Advanced reservations are suggested for all tours, and space can be reserved in person or by phone (☎ **209/372-1240**). Double-check at tour desks for updated departure schedules and prices. Most of the tours leave from Yosemite Lodge.

The **Valley Floor Tour** is a great way to get acclimated. It's a 2-hour ride in either an open-air tram or an enclosed motorcoach, depending on the weather. The cost is $17 per person, $8.50 for children, and $15 for seniors. Trams depart from Yosemite Village, the Ahwahnee, Yosemite Lodge, and Curry Village every half hour daily (hours change from winter to summer). The trip includes a good selection of photo ops, such as El Capitan, Tunnel View, and Half Dome. A guide leads a historical, geological, and informative discussion from a pulpit at the head of the tram. This ride is also available on nights when the moon is full or near full. It's an eerie but beautiful scene. Moonlight illuminates the valley's granite walls and gives visitors a rare picture of Yosemite. Blankets and hot cocoa are provided. Dress warmly, though, because it can get mighty chilly after the sun goes down. On the other hand, if you take this trip during the day, wear sunscreen.

The **Glacier Point Tour** is a 4-hour scenic bus ride through the valley to Glacier Point. The round-trip cost is $20 for adults, $19.25 for seniors, and $10.25 for children. Buses depart Yosemite Lodge, the Ahwahnee, Yosemite Village, and Curry Village daily at 10am and 1:30pm. One-way trips are also available for hikers on foot. The cost is $10 for adults and seniors, and $5 for children. One-way fares leave Yosemite Lodge at 8:30am, 10am, and 1:30pm daily. Buses depart Glacier Point at 10am, noon, and 3:30pm. Reservations must be made at least 1 day ahead of time. All Glacier Point buses are available in spring through fall only.

Tours also depart from Yosemite Valley to **Mariposa Grove** (see chapter 4). The trip takes 6 hours and costs $34 for adults and $18 for children. Buses depart Yosemite Lodge at 9:30am daily. The trip includes the Big Trees tram tour that winds through the grove and stops for lunch at Wawona (lunch is not provided). You can combine the trip to Glacier Point and Mariposa Grove in an 8-hour bus ride that costs $44.50 for adults and $25 for children. Buses depart Yosemite Lodge at 9:30am daily.

Buses also depart Yosemite Valley for **Tuolumne Meadows** (see chapter 4), although they don't allow for much time to explore, unless you arrange to stay overnight. It's an all-day trip, with stops along the way. The cost is $20 for adults and seniors, $10.25 for children. You can also jump off at any point along the way and the fare will be reduced.

Spring through fall, the Yosemite Theater offers inexpensive theatrical and musical programs designed to supplement Park Service programs. These tend to repeat from year to year, but old favorites include a conversation with John Muir, a film on Yosemite's future, and sing-alongs. Inquire at the Valley Visitor Center.

# 4

# Hikes & Other Outdoor Pursuits in Yosemite

*Y*osemite is a nature lover's paradise, filled with a myriad of activities to keep you from ever getting bored. Always remember, when preparing for a hike, pack more water and food than the hike alone requires—it's very easy to get sidetracked.

## 1 Day Hikes & Scenic Walks

Below is a selection of day hikes throughout Yosemite National Park. Distances and times are round-trip estimates unless otherwise noted.

### IN & NEAR THE VALLEY

**Mirror Lake.** 2.6 miles/1–4 hours. Easy. Take the shuttle bus to stop No. 17 or 18 and follow the signs.

A half-mile paved trail climbs about 60 feet along the west side of Tenaya Creek to Mirror Lake, aptly named because the still surface reflects the overhanging granite above. The trail connects with a beautiful 3-mile loop around the lake, which was recently restored.

**Lower Yosemite Fall.** 0.5 miles/30 minutes. Easy. Take the shuttle bus to stop No. 7. Follow the paved path from the Yosemite Fall parking area to the base of this waterfall.

Be prepared to get damp. Lower Yosemite Fall reaches 320 feet, but it packs the accumulated punch of the entire 2,425-foot waterfall. You can also take this trip from Yosemite Village by following the path from the Valley Visitor Center to the Yosemite Fall parking area. Add another half-mile or 40 minutes each way. This walk is wheelchair accessible with assistance.

**Upper Yosemite Fall.** 7.2 miles/6–8 hours. Strenuous. Take the shuttle bus to stop No. 8. The trailhead is next to Sunnyside Walk-in Campground, behind Yosemite Lodge.

Up, up, and away. Climbing 2,700 feet and offering spectacular views from the ledge above, this hike is not for the faint of heart. Take it slow, rest often, and absorb the scenery as you climb

# Hiking Trails Near Yosemite Valley

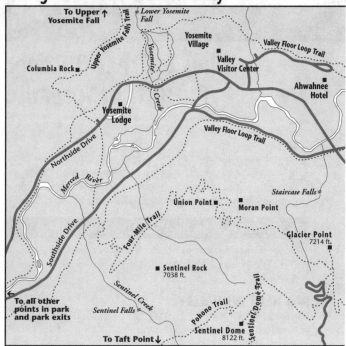

higher and higher above the valley. One mile up, you'll reach Columbia Point, which offers a panoramic view. The rest of the trail dips and climbs, with ample opportunity for cooling off beneath the spray from the fall above. The last quarter-mile is a series of torturous, seemingly endless switchbacks that ascend through underbrush before opening at a clearing near the top of the fall. The view from here inspires vertigo. It's a worthwhile walk upstream to see the creek before it takes a half-mile tumble to the valley floor below. You can also stay overnight up here, with proper permits and equipment. See chapter 5.

**Columbia Rock.** 2 miles/2–3 hours. Moderate. Use the trailhead for Upper Yosemite Fall.

The hike mirrors the beginning ascent of the waterfall trail but stops at Columbia Rock, 1,000 feet above the valley. There's no valley view from here, but the sights are still impressive. Because it's on the sunny side of the valley, it's also less likely to get an accumulation of snow.

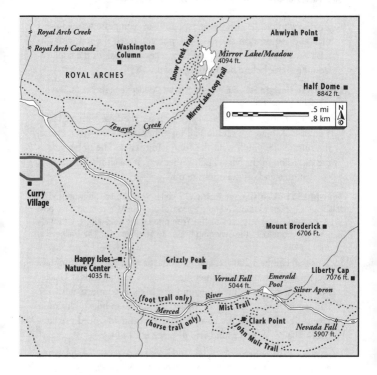

**Base of Bridalveil Fall.** 0.5 miles/30 minutes. Easy. Drive or walk to the Bridalveil Fall parking area, about 3 miles west of Yosemite Village. Follow trail markers.

Bridalveil Fall drops 620 feet from top to bottom. In the spring, expect to get wet. This walk is wheelchair accessible with assistance.

**Mist Trail to Vernal Fall.** 3 miles/2–3 hours. Moderate to strenuous. Take the shuttle bus to stop No. 16 and walk to the Happy Isles Bridge. Cross the bridge and follow the signs to the trail.

This hike begins on the famous 211-mile John Muir Trail to Mt. Whitney in Sequoia/Kings Canyon National Park. From the Happy Isles Bridge, the trail climbs 400 feet to the Vernal Fall Bridge, which has a good view of what lies ahead, as well as water and rest rooms. The rest of the climb requires a choice. You can either take a series of switchbacks along the side of the mountain and come out above the fall, or ascend the Mist Trail (our suggestion), which is a steep climb with 500 steps—it's wet, picturesque, and refreshing. The Mist Trail is so named because the spray from the fall drenches anyone who tackles this route, especially in spring. Be warned—it's slick and requires cautious steps. Once you reach the top, you can relax on a series of smooth granite beaches and soak in the cool, refreshing water before hiking back down.

**Onward to Nevada Fall.** 6.8 miles/6–8 hours. Moderate to strenuous. Use the trailhead for Vernal Fall.

This trip mirrors the Vernal Fall climb for the first 3 miles. From Vernal Fall, hike to Nevada Fall on either side of the river. Along the south side, you'll walk the John Muir Trail. The north side is the extension of the Mist Trail. Either way, it's a climb. For variety, you can descend on the opposite trail.

**Four-Mile Trail to Glacier Point.** 9.6 miles/7–10 hours. Strenuous. The trailhead is 1.25 miles from Yosemite Village, at the Four Mile parking area, post V-18, or take the shuttle bus to the Yosemite Lodge stop No. 8 and walk behind the Lodge over the Swinging Bridge to Southeast Dr. The trailhead is ¹/4 mile west.

This trail climbs 3,200 feet and has some terrific views (okay, so does every trail climbing out of Yosemite Valley). This trail ends at Glacier Point, but if you'd like to extend the hike, it connects with the Panorama Trail at the end. However, if you plan to hike both simultaneously, it may require an overnight stay and advanced preparation—the combined round-trip distance is 14 miles.

**Panorama Trail.** 9 miles one-way/6–10 hours. Moderate to strenuous. The hike begins at Glacier Point, at the east end of the parking area.

From Glacier Point, this trail drops 3,200 feet, but somehow it still feels like a climb. At one of the prettiest points, it crosses Illilouette Fall about 1.5 miles from Glacier Point. It continues along the Panorama Cliffs and eventually winds up at Nevada Fall, where it's a straight descent to Yosemite Valley via the Mist or John Muir trails. You can hike this trail in conjunction with the Four-Mile Trail, but it might entail an overnight stop. It's also possible to take the bus to Glacier Point and only hike one-way.

**Half Dome.** 16.5 miles/10–14 hours. Moderate to strenuous. Take the shuttle bus to stop No. 16 at Happy Isles.

This long, steep trip climbs 4,900 feet. From Happy Isles, take the John Muir Trail past Vernal and Nevada falls, and through Little Yosemite Valley. Leave the John Muir Trail for the Half Dome Trail and look for a natural spring atop a short spur. Fill up here because this is the last water on the way up. The last 200 feet of hiking up the back of Half Dome require the use of cables. And a strong heart wouldn't hurt. Half Dome is amazingly level on top. Hiking this rock is a divisive issue. Some question why humans are so compelled to conquer every summit. Others say because it's there. A lot of people agree. An estimated 600 people climb Half Dome every day in the summer. It's possible to cut the length by beginning in Little Yosemite Valley (you'll need a wilderness permit to camp here).

## SOUTH OF THE VALLEY

**Chilnualna Falls from Wawona.** 8 miles/6 hours. Strenuous. Enter Yosemite National Park on Hwy. 41 and continue north. Turn right on Chilnualna Rd., just north of the Merced River's south fork. Stay on this road until it dead-ends at "The Redwoods," about 1.3 miles. This is the trailhead.

One of the tallest outside Yosemite Valley, the fall cascades down two chutes. The one at the bottom is narrow and packs a real punch after a wet winter. A series of switchbacks leads to the top fall, and from here you can hike to Bridalveil Campground, or continue on to Chilnualna Lakes. If you plan to hike to the lakes, this is a great place to stay overnight, but don't forget your wilderness permit. Also remember to pack a swimsuit—there are a few swimming holes at the base of the waterfalls.

**Chilnualna Falls from Bridalveil Fall.** 18.8 miles/9 hours. Moderate to strenuous. Take Hwy. 41 to Glacier Point Rd. and turn east. Take Glacier Point Rd. to the trailhead at Bridalveil Campground.

The trail treks along gentle grades through forests at first, then turns up toward Turner Meadows. It's a scenic trip without Yosemite's summer crowds. It offers pretty views as the trail wanders near overlooks along the route to the falls.

**Grizzly Giant.** 1.6 miles/1 1/2 hours. Easy. The trail begins at a sign near the map dispenser at the east end of the Mariposa Grove parking lot.

This is the walking alternative to the Mariposa Grove tram tour described on page 46. It's a nice stroll to see an impressive tree and the hike only climbs 400 feet.

**Mariposa Grove.** 13 miles/1 long day. Moderate to strenuous. Park at the Wawona Store parking area and walk east 1/4 mile to Forest Dr. The trailhead is on the right.

It sounds long, but there is a one-way option in the summer that utilizes the Wawona shuttle bus service on the return trip. This hike is a nice alternative to the crowded drive to Mariposa Grove. It climbs through a forest, then ascends the Wawona Dome and Wawona Basin, both of which provide excellent views.

**Ostrander Lake.** 12.8 miles/6 hours. Moderate to strenuous. Take Hwy. 41 to Glacier Point Rd. and turn east. Take Glacier Point Rd. to the trailhead about 1.3 miles past Bridalveil Campground, on the right-hand side of the road.

The trail begins on an abandoned road. It winds through evidence of a forest fire until it reaches Bear Meadow. It begins to climb after crossing Bridalveil Creek and crosses several ridges before reaching the lake. The best camping is reportedly on the lake's west end. Ostrander Lake is popular in summer and during winter as a cross-country ski spot. The Sierra Club also manages the nearby Ostrander Hut.

**Sentinel Dome.** 2.2 miles/2–3 hours. Moderate. Take Glacier Point Rd. to the Sentinel Dome parking lot, about 3 miles from Glacier Point.

You'll be able to see Sentinel Dome on your left. The trail descends slightly, and at the first fork bear right. The trail winds through manzanita and pine before beginning its ascent. It's a steep scramble to the top of Sentinel Dome and you have to leave the trail on the north side in order to scramble up. The view from the top offers a 180° panorama of Yosemite Valley that includes a host of impressive and recognizable geologic landmarks.

**Taft Point.** 2.2 miles/2 hours. Easy. The trailhead begins at the same point as the hike to Sentinel Dome. At the fork, head left.

The walk to Taft Point is undemanding. It crosses a broad meadow dotted in early summer by wildflowers. Near Taft Point, note the deep chasms in the rock, known as the "fissures." Some of the cracks are 40 feet long and 20 feet wide at the top and 100 feet deep. The wall of Yosemite actually overhangs the narrow ravine below, and if you carefully peer over the cliff, note that your head is on the opposite side of a stream running far beneath you. A small pipe railing further on marks the 6-by-3-foot Taft Point overlook hanging over Yosemite Valley.

**Wawona Meadow Loop.** 3.5 miles/1$^1$/2 hours. Easy. Take the paved road through the golf course on the west side of Hwy. 41, and walk about 50 yards to the trail.

This relaxing stroll encircles Wawona Meadow, curving around at its east end and heading back toward the road. It crosses the highway and winds through forest until it returns at the Wawona Hotel. Some cars still use this road, so watch out.

**Wawona Point.** 1 mile/1 hour. Easy. Take the tram tour at Mariposa Grove to the Wawona Tunnel Tree and exit.

Hike back to the north, toward Wawona, and follow a spur road at the Galen Clark Tree. From here you can see the entire Wawona Basin, a view only available to those who venture out on foot.

## NORTH OF THE VALLEY

**Cathedral Lakes.** 8 miles/4–6 hours. Moderate. The trailhead is at the west end of Tuolumne Meadows, west of Budd Creek. Take the shuttle bus in summer to avoid parking problems.

These lakes are set in granite bowls cut by glaciers. The peaks and domes around both Lower and Upper Cathedral lakes are worth the hike alone. Lower Cathedral Lake is next to Cathedral Peak and is a good place to stop for a snack before heading up the hill to enjoy the upper lake.

**Cloud's Rest.** 14 miles/7 hours. Moderate. Take Hwy. 120 to Tenaya Lake. The trailhead begins at a campground parking lot down a closed road that crosses an outlet of the lake.

This hike descends through a wooded area. Head toward Sunrise Lake. Ascend out of Tenaya Canyon and at a junction bear right (this part of the trail is usually well signed). Views begin almost at once. Your destination is clear, which is a good thing since the trail is sketchy at this point. The last scramble to the top is a little spooky, with sheer drops on each side. Yosemite River is on the right and the Little Yosemite is on the left. Bravery is rewarded with spectacular views of the park's granite domes. Overnight stays are rewarded with beautiful sunrises.

**Dog Lake.** 3 miles/3 hours. Easy. Take Hwy. 120 to the access road for Tuolumne Lodge. Pass the ranger station and park at a parking lot on the left. Walk north up an embankment and recross the highway to find Dog Lake Trail.

It's an easy climb through forests with great views of Mt. Dana. Dog Lake is warm, shallow, and great for swimming.

**El Capitan (the back way).** 14.4 miles/6 hours. Strenuous. Take Hwy. 120 to the Tamarack Flat Campground. Turn right and follow the road to the east end of the campground, where you'll see an abandoned road. The trail begins here.

Trek along the abandoned road to Cascade Creek and then along a roadbed to the North Rim Trail. Prepare for switchbacks. The trail climbs and climbs and climbs to a summit, where it hits a spur trail. Take the spur to the summit to enjoy the views. (The main trail heads to Eagle Peak.) Be careful. Punishment for carelessness is a poorly rated one-way trip to the valley floor.

# Backcountry Hikes in Yosemite

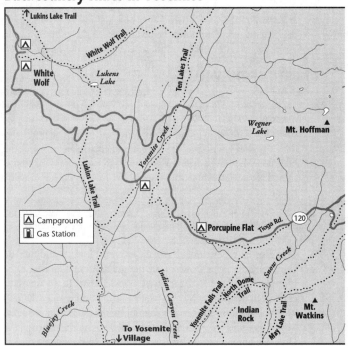

**Elizabeth Lake.** 6 miles/3 hours. Moderate. Take Hwy. 120 to the group camping area of Tuolumne Meadows Campground, where the trail begins.

This popular day hike attracts a slew of people, which can be a bummer, but it's magnificent nonetheless for its beauty. Elizabeth Lake glistens like ice. Don't forget your camera and some extra film—the entire route is one long Kodak moment.

**Gaylor Lakes.** 6 miles/3 hours. Moderate. Take Hwy. 120 to Tioga Pass. The trailhead is on the northwest side of the road.

This trail begins with a climb, then descends to the alpine lake. It's a particularly pretty hike in early summer, when the mountainsides are dotted with wildflowers.

**Glacier Canyon to Dana Lake.** 4.6 miles/2 hours. Moderate to strenuous. Take Hwy. 120 to Tioga Lake. The trailhead is on the west side of the lake, about a mile east of the pass.

This is a less-crowded alternative to the above hike to Mt. Dana that doesn't top the mountain, although that option is available for

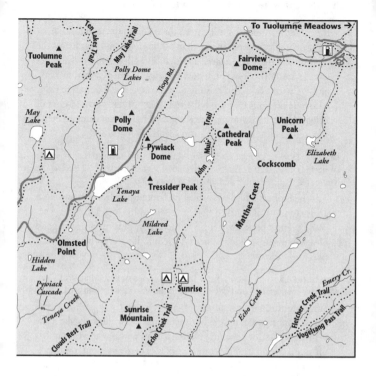

experienced hikers. The trail begins at the Ansel Adams Wilderness and is not maintained, although it is fairly visible. This area is easily damaged, so be sure to tread lightly. The route leads through the headway of Glacier Canyon to Dana Lake, which is fed by glaciers. Mt. Dana looms large from the lake's shore.

**Glen Aulin.** 10.4 miles/1 long day. Moderate to strenuous. Take Hwy. 120 toward Tuolumne Meadows, about 1 mile east of the Tuolumne Meadows Visitor Center and just a few yards east of the bridge over the Tuolumne River. Follow a marked turnoff and take the paved road on your left. The trailhead begins about 0.3 miles ahead, at a road that turns right and heads up a hill toward the stables.

Start hiking across a flat meadow toward Soda Springs and Glen Aulin. The trail is well marked and signs along the way do a good job of pointing out the area's history. This was once the old Tioga Road, which was built in 1883 to serve the Great Sierra Mine in Tioga Pass. This walk offers a view to the landmarks of Tuolumne Meadows. Lembert Dome rises behind you almost 900 feet above the meadow. About 0.4 miles from the trailhead the road forks; head right up a grassy slope. In less than 500 feet is a trail that leaves the road on the right and a steel sign that says Glen Aulin is 4.7 miles ahead. Along the way you'll pass Fairview Dome, Cathedral Peak, and Unicorn Peak. The crashing noise you hear is Tuolumne Falls, a cascade of water that drops 12 feet, then 40 feet down a series of ledges. From here you can see a nearby High Sierra camp. There's also a hikers' camp if you want to spend the night.

**Lembert Dome.** 2.8 miles/2–3 hours. Moderate. The trailhead is at a parking lot north of Hwy. 120 in Tuolumne Meadows at road marker T-32. Follow the nature trail that starts here and take off at marker No. 2.

This hike offers a bird's-eye view of Tuolumne Meadows and it's a great vista. A well-marked trail leads you to the top, and from there you'll see the peaks that encircle the valley, plus get a pretty good idea of how the meadow system is laid out. It's a great place for sunrises and sunsets.

**May Lake.** 2.5 miles/3 hours. Easy. Take Hwy. 120 east past White Wolf. Turn off at road marker T-21 and drive 2 miles to the May Lake parking area.

Winding through forests and granite, this picturesque hike offers ample opportunities to fish, but swimming is not allowed. May Lake is in the center of Yosemite National Park and is a good jumping-off point for other high country hikes. There are numerous peaks surrounding the lake, including the 10,855-foot-high Mt. Hoffman, which rises behind the lake. There is a High Sierra camp here as well, and a hikers' camp on the south side of the lake.

**Mono Pass.** 8.5 miles/4–6 hours. Moderate to strenuous. The trailhead for this hike is on the south side of Hwy. 120 as you enter the park from Lee Vining. Drive about 1.5 miles from the park entrance to Dana Meadows, where the trail begins on an abandoned road and up alongside Parker Creek Pass.

You'll pass some historic cabin sites, then hike down to Walker Lake, and return via the same route. The hike loops into the Inyo National Forest and the Ansel Adams Wilderness, and climbs to an altitude of 10,600 feet.

**Mt. Dana.** 5.8 miles/5 hours. Strenuous. The trailhead is on the southeast side of Hwy. 120 at Tioga Pass.

This climb is an in-your-face reminder that Mt. Dana is Yosemite's second highest peak. The mountain rises 13,053 feet and the trail gains a whopping 3,100 feet in 3 miles. The views at the top are wonderful, once you're able to stand upright after catching your breath. You can see Mono Lake from the summit. In summer, the wildflowers add to this hike's beauty.

**North Dome.** 10 miles/5 hours. Easy to moderate. Take Hwy. 120 east to the Porcupine Flat Campground, past White Wolf. About 1 mile past the campground is a sign for Porcupine Creek at a closed road. Park in the designated area.

Walk south down the abandoned road toward the Porcupine Creek Campground. A mile past the campground the trail hits a junction with the Tenaya Creek and Tuolumne Meadows Trail. Pass a junction toward Yosemite Falls and head uphill toward North Dome. The ascent is treacherous due to loose gravel, but from the top you'll catch an all-encompassing view of Yosemite Valley, second only to the view from Half Dome.

**Polly Dome Lake.** 12.5 miles/6 hours. Easy to moderate. Take Hwy. 120 past White Wolf to Tenaya Lake. Drive about $^1/_2$ mile to a picnic area midway along the lake. The trailhead is across the road from the picnic area.

This hike is easily the road least traveled. The trip to Polly Dome Lake is a breeze and you'll find nary another traveler in sight. There are several lakes beneath Polly Dome that can accommodate camping. The trail fades in and out, so watch for markers. It crosses a rocky area en route, then skirts southeast at a pond just after the rocky section. Polly Dome Lake is at the base of—you guessed it— Polly Dome, a visual aid to help hikers stay the course.

**Soda Springs.** 1.5 miles/1–2 hours. Easy. 2 trailheads: 1 is at a crosswalk just east of the Tuolumne Meadows Visitor Center. The other leaves from a parking lot north of Hwy. 120 at road marker T-32. Follow the gravel road around a locked gate.

This trail crosses Tuolumne Meadows, then Tuolumne River on a wooden bridge. It's peaceful and beautiful, the sound of the river gurgling along as it winds slowly through the wide expanse of Tuolumne Meadows. The trail heads to a carbonated spring where you can taste the water, although it gets mixed reviews. For years, the spring was administered and owned by the Sierra Club, which operates the nearby Parsons Lodge, now an activity center. Also nearby is the historic McCauley Cabin, which is now a ranger's residence.

**Sunrise Lakes.** 7–8 miles/5–8 hours. Moderate to strenuous. Take Hwy. 120 to Tenaya Lake. The trail begins in the parking area on the east side of the road near the southwest end of the lake.

Look for a sign that says SUNRISE. Follow the level road to Tenaya Creek. Cross the creek and follow the trail to the right. The hike parallels Tenaya Creek for about a quarter-mile, then moves away through a wooded area and climbs gently up a rocky rise. After a while the trail descends quickly to the outlet of Mildred Lake. You'll be able to see Mt. Hoffmann, Tuolumne Peak, and Tenaya Canyon. At the halfway mark, the trail passes through a hemlock grove, then comes to a junction. Head left. (The trail on the right goes toward Cloud's Rest.) About a quarter-mile from the junction you'll reach Lower Sunrise Lake, tucked into the slope of Sunrise Mountain. The trail climbs past Middle Sunrise Lake and continues upward along a cascading creek coming from Upper Sunrise Lake. The trail follows the lake's shore and opens in less than a half-mile onto a wide, bare sandy pass. It's all downhill from here. Before you is the snowcapped Clark Range. The trail begins its descent, sharply switching back and forth in some places. There is a High Sierra camp and backpackers' camp here as well.

**Vogelsang.** 14.4 miles/1 day. Moderate to strenuous. Take Hwy. 120 to Tuolumne Meadows and watch for the signed trailhead for the John Muir Trail and Lyell Fork.

The trail goes south through the woods to a footbridge over the Dana Fork. Cross the bridge and follow the John Muir Trail upstream. Go right at the next fork. The trail crosses the Lyell Fork by footbridge. Take the left fork a couple hundred feet ahead. Continue onward and just before you cross the bridge at Rafferty Creek you'll reach another junction. Veer right and prepare for switchbacks up a rocky slope. The trail climbs steeply for about a quarter-mile then levels off as it darts toward and away from Rafferty Creek for the next 4 miles. The trail gradually ascends to Tuolumne Pass, crossing many small creeks and tributaries en route. Two small tarns mark the pass. One drains south and the other north. Just south of the tarns the trail splits. Veer left. (The right fork offers a 2-mile round-trip jaunt to Boothe Lake.) You'll climb to a meadow with great views, and here, at 10,180 feet, you'll reach the highest of Yosemite's High Sierra camps. It's very pretty, with a great location—the base of Fletcher Peak, on the banks of Fletcher Creek and close to Fletcher Lake.

## 2  Other Sports & Activities

About the only thing you can't do in Yosemite is surf. In addition to sightseeing, Yosemite is a great place to bike, ski, rock climb, fish, even golf—all of which sort of serves as a reminder that while here you really aren't getting away from it all.

**BACKPACKING**   Guided tours range from simple walks to multiday excursions into Yosemite's backcountry and can be arranged by phone (☎ 209/372-8344). Techniques and skills are taught along the way. Meals are included on longer trips. The instructor-to-student ratio does not exceed 7 to 1. Private trips are available, as is transportation to and from the trailhead. Three-day trips ascend Mt. Lyell or hike from Young Lakes to Mt. Conness. Four-day excursions travel from Ten Lakes to Tuolumne Meadows, or from Tuolumne Meadows to Yosemite Valley.

**BICYCLING**   Bikes may be rented by the hour ($5.25) or the day ($20) at Curry Village or Yosemite Lodge. Both shops are open from 8am to 7pm daily, but the Curry Village shop closes in winter. Hours may vary slightly depending on weather and the season. Information is also available by phone (☎ 209/372-8367 or 209/372-8319). Helmets are required for all riders under age 18 and are provided to riders of all ages free of charge. Cyclists benefit from having access to special bikeways, as well as shuttle bus roads and thoroughfares for general traffic.

**CROSS-COUNTRY SKIING**   Excursions are led from Badger Pass and Glacier Point. Information is available by phone (☎ 209/372-8444). Learn to telemark, snow camp, or take an overnight expedition.

**FISHING**   General information is available from the California State Department of Fish and Game (☎ 209/222-3761) or the U.S. Army Corps of Engineers (☎ 209/689-3255). Yosemite Creek Outfitters leads fly-fishing trips in Yosemite (☎ 209/962-5060). The Groveland-based organization offers everything from 1-day fly-fishing lessons to multiday excursions on horseback or by whitewater raft. You can also make custom arrangements.

**GOLF**   Wawona sports a 9-hole golf course designed in 1917 by noted course designer Walter G. Fovarque, who laid out many courses in Japan. The par-35 course is 3,050 yards long and alternates between meadows and fairways. You can book your tee time by phone (☎ 209/375-6572). There are several other courses just outside the park. The River Creek Golf Course (☎ 209/683-3388) is in the small hamlet of Ahwahnee (not the hotel). And just to add to the confusion, the Ahwahnee Golf Course (☎ 209/642-1343) is in Oakhurst.

**HORSEBACK RIDING**   Yosemite Valley phased out its stables in 1997, although pack animals and private stock may still board there. Stables remain at Wawona, and at Tuolumne Meadows in summer only. Reservations can be made by phone (☎ 209/372-8427 or 209/372-8348). Guided backcountry pack trips are also available with advanced reservations from May to September. These 4- to 6-day saddle trips lead to Yosemite's High Sierra camps. The cost is $550 to $900 including meals. Yosemite Trails Pack Station (☎ **209/683-7611** or 209/683-9122) offers riding just south of Wawona. Minarets Pack Station (☎ **209/868-3405**) is in the High Sierra and leads day trips to Yosemite and the Ansel Adams Wilderness. You may also try the horses at the Bohna Arena (☎ **209/ 683-2817**).

**ICE-SKATING**   The ice rink at Curry Village is open from early November to March, weather permitting. One session costs $5 for adults and $4.50 for children. Skate rental is another $2. Session hours are noon to 2:30pm, 3:30 to 6pm, and 7 to 9:30pm daily. The rink also offers morning sessions from 8:30 to 11am on weekends.

**RAFTING**   A raft rental shop is located at Curry Village (☎ **209/ 372-8341**). Daily rental fees are $12.50 for adults, $10.50 for children under 13. Fees include a raft, paddles, mandatory life preservers, and transportation from El Capitan back to Curry Village.

**ROCK CLIMBING**   No guidebook would be complete without mentioning Yosemite's famous rock-climbing school. The park is considered one of the world's premier climbing grounds. The **Yosemite Mountaineering School** (☎ 209/372-8344) provides experienced instruction for beginning, intermediate, and advanced climbers in the valley and Tuolumne Meadows. Classes last anywhere from a day to a week. Private lessons are also available. All equipment is provided and rates vary according to the class or program.

**SKIING**   Yosemite's **Badger Pass** is open from Thanksgiving through Easter Sunday. Year-round information is available by phone (☎ **209/372-1446**). There are special programs for kids, including a daylong child care/ski school called Badger Pups. *Tip:* You can ski for free Sunday through Thursday by staying overnight in one of the accommodations operated by Yosemite Concession Services.

Twenty-two miles from the valley, Badger Pass was established in 1935. It's a small resort with nine runs, four lifts, and a chairlift. It's geared toward intermediate skiers and is reputed to be an excellent place to learn to ski. Its reputation rests squarely on the shoulders of Nic Fiore, a Yosemite ski legend who arrived in the park in 1947 to ski for a season and never left. Fiore became director of the ski school in 1956. Park officials credit Fiore with making Badger Pass what it is today—a family and teaching area where old-world tradition lives on.

**ESPECIALLY FOR KIDS**   Many of the activities listed above have special programs for children, including rock-climbing and ski lessons. In addition, Yosemite offers a Junior and Senior Ranger program and special walks and lectures. All are described in chapter 2, under "Tips for Travelers with Children."

## 3   Exploring the Backcountry

Of the more than 4 million people who visit Yosemite each year, 95% never leave the valley. Our hint: Leave the valley—the brave 5% who do are well rewarded. A wild, lonelier Yosemite awaits just a few miles from the crowds. Here, you'll find some of the most grandiose landscape in the Sierra. But most hikers head for Tuolumne Meadows, the high country and a backpacking paradise. Tioga Pass via Highway 120 is the gateway to the high country. Once through the pass, the high country presents meadows of wildflowers, stark granite domes, and shimmering rivers and lakes. There is a campground that makes a nice alternative to the valley's summer crowds, but it tends to fill up in summer, too. A car is more vital in Yosemite's high country. There is a once-a-day shuttle from the valley to Tuolumne Meadows. The bus leaves the valley at 8am and will let you off anywhere along the route. The driver waits in Tuolumne Meadows for 2 hours before heading back to the valley, where the bus arrives at about 4pm. The fare is $12 one-way, slightly less for those who hop off midway. In addition, the park offers a summer-only shuttle bus in Tuolumne Meadows.

Tuolumne Meadows is an enormous meadow bordered by the Tuolumne River and a wall of granite cliffs. Several peaks rise high above and offer challenging hiking and rock climbing. In spring and midsummer, the meadow fills with wildflowers and turns an emerald green. Fishing in the river is popular. A number of hikes begin in the area. There is also a general store that stocks last-minute hiking supplies, a slough of canvas tent-cabins (often all full in summer), and a restaurant with pricey but good food.

In addition to Tuolumne Meadows, Tenaya Lake is a beautiful destination spot en route that offers a site for canoeing, hiking, fishing, and sailing. The water is like ice and it's set in a bowl of granite, surrounded by sheer slopes. Many hikes lead from here to the high country. There's ample parking and picnic spots available. White Wolf is about midway between the valley and Tuolumne Meadows. It consists of a campground, canvas tent-cabins, a small store, and a restaurant. The scenery here is less dramatic, although it serves as a starting point for many hikers. Much of this region is accessible only by snowshoe in the winter.

Like any backcountry experience, staying here—or anyplace outside the valley—requires advanced planning, and if you're a beginner, a reasonable itinerary. Planning a 5-day excursion your first time out wouldn't be wise. But an overnighter, or 2 nights out, is reasonable and Yosemite has hikes that can accommodate and reward those who venture—even briefly—off the well-paved path.

In addition, the park has five High Sierra camps that provide food and shelter, allowing hikers to shun heavy backpacking gear with the knowledge that someone a few miles ahead has everything under control. All fill quickly and advanced reservations are necessary. The camps—May Lake, Glen Aulin, Vogelsang, Sunrise Lakes, Merced Lake, and Tuolumne, are situated about a day's walk apart. Each camp is a rustic resort. Tent-cabins are furnished with steel bunk beds, wood stoves, and folding table and chairs. Beds include a mattress, three blankets, a comforter, and pillow. A towel, washcloth, soap, and candles are also provided. Most tents sleep four, but some accommodate only two people. It means you'll often be sharing your tent with strangers, but the camps tend to attract people who rank high on the camaraderie scale, so that's not usually a problem. Breakfast and dinner are served family style in a dining tent. The food is yummy and portions are generous. One dinner meal included pasta, filet mignon, soup and salad, eggplant Parmesan, and cookies. Breakfast is usually juice, coffee, fruit, scrambled eggs, bacon, pancakes, and muffins or biscuits. Box lunches are available for an additional charge. All you need to bring is day-hike stuff, plus a flashlight, personal toiletries, something to sleep in, a change of underclothes, and bed linen.

Each camp accommodates 30 to 50 guests and demand exceeds supply, so accommodations are assigned by a lottery. Requests are accepted in fall and assigned in winter to the lucky few. Cancellations are frequent, however, so it's worth a last-minute call to see if space is available at any of the camps. In addition, the camps offer a meals-only option (reservations required) if you want to bring your own tent, etc., and eat at the camp. To request an application for

High Sierra camp accommodations call ☎ **209/252-4848** or 209/454-2002. The latter number also has an extensive amount of information available by Touch-Tone phone. Applications are accepted September 1 to November 30. The lottery drawing is held in mid-December and guests are notified by mid-March.

## PREPARING FOR YOUR BACKCOUNTRY TRIP

Most importantly, get a detailed topographical map at the onset of any overnight hike. They are available from the U.S. Geological Survey and can be obtained by writing to the USGS's western distribution branch at Box 25286, Federal Center, Denver, CO 80225. Maps are also available at many Yosemite stores, visitor centers, ranger stations, and the Wilderness Center in Yosemite Valley.

**Permits & Fees**    All overnight backpacking stays require a wilderness permit, available by phone, mail, or at one of four locations in the park. Permits can be reserved 2 days to 4 months in advance. Permits cost $3 to process. Reservations are accepted every year, usually beginning in late winter. Call ☎ **209/372-0740** or write to Wilderness Permits, P.O. Box 545, Yosemite National Park, CA 95389.

If advanced planning isn't your style, first-come first-served permits are available up to 24 hours prior to your trip. Permit stations are located at the Yosemite Valley Visitor Center, Wawona Information Station, and Big Oak Flat Information Station in Tuolumne Meadows in summer. The popular trails such as Half Dome, Little Yosemite Valley, and Cloud's Rest fill up early. Call ☎ **209/372-0200** for open permit station locations and hours.

To get a permit you must provide a name, address, telephone number, the number of people in your party, the method of travel (snowshoe, horse, foot), number of stock if applicable, start and end dates, start and end trailheads, and principal destination. Include alternate dates and trailheads as well.

**Special Regulations & Etiquette**    Campfires are not allowed above 9,600 feet in Yosemite. Don't leave anything behind but footprints. Backpackers are strongly encouraged to have a bear canister for storing food, especially on the better-traveled routes. Canisters can be rented for $3 a day at the Yosemite Valley Sports Shop.

## OVERNIGHT HIKES

All hikers should purchase a good topographical map before embarking on any overnight hike. These are available at stores, visitor centers, and ranger stations throughout Yosemite National Park. In addition, bears frequent the high country, so stay alert. In the summer months, mosquitoes are public enemy number one, so bring plenty of repellent. Also pack sunscreen since much of Yosemite's high country is on granite, above the tree line. Stay off of high peaks during thunderstorms and don't attempt any climb if it looks as if a storm is rolling in. The peaks are magnets for lightening. And finally, trailheads along Tioga Road are accessible only by snowshoe in winter as the road is usually closed from November until May.

**Chilnualna Lakes/Buena Vista Peak Loop.** 28 miles/4 days. Moderate to strenuous. Take Hwy. 41 to Wawona in Yosemite National Park. Turn east on Chilnualna Rd. and stay on this road for about 1.3 miles until you reach "The Redwoods," where the road ends. This is the trailhead.

The first day's hike is 8 miles, to Chilnualna Falls, one of the park's tallest falls outside the valley. It's a strenuous climb up. The falls tumble down a narrow chute and 50 feet up is another fall, which can be quite a vision in spring with a strong winter runoff. Above the falls the trail ascends via switchbacks up a gorge to a junction. One route will lead through forests toward Bridalveil Campground, the other toward Chilnualna Lakes. Just below this junction are several nice places to camp overnight. There are also a number of nearby swimming holes. From here, it's a climb along the headwaters of the creek to a set of high-altitude lakes. About 2.5 miles up is Grouse Lake Creek. This can be a tough cross during high water and the rock is very slick. Head north and left after the crossing toward Turner Meadows for about a half-mile. At the next junction, head right and east toward Chilnualna Lakes, about 5 miles away. Buena Vista Peak rises above the lakes. Campsites are plentiful in this area. From the lakes, head up into the 9,040-foot Buena Vista Pass. At the pass, head south on Buena Vista Trail toward Royal Arch Lake. The next junction goes right and west toward Johnson, Crescent, and Grouse lakes. After Grouse Lake is the Grouse Lake Creek crossing and the return trail to Chilnualna Falls and the parking area.

**Ten Lakes Basin.** 12.8 miles/2 days. Moderate. On Hwy. 120 east, pass the White Wolf Campground to the trailhead parking lot, just before a bridge and Yosemite Creek sign. The trailhead is on the north side of the road.

The trail is well marked and picturesque, with lots of rocks to climb around and lakes for swimming. You'll stay on the Ten Lakes Trail the entire distance to the first lake and beyond. Follow the signs. The trail also offers some great fishing for brook and rainbow trout. Mosquitoes can be a major deterrent in summer.

## Backpacking for Beginners

The longer the trip, the more planning it requires. In general, backpacking requires more preparation than any other sport, plus minute attention to detail. Everything you need for food, clothing, and shelter must be carried with you. It's important to be thorough but conscientious when it comes to weight. First and foremost, the most important gear is what's on your back and on your feet—good boots and a sturdy pack are a necessity. You'll also need a good sleeping bag and sleeping pad. Packs generally come in two types: internal and external frames. Opinions vary over which is best, but external frame packs are slightly cheaper, and internal frame packs are better for long distances or trails that twist and turn. These packs more evenly distribute weight and cinch tight across your hips, making them more comfortable for long hauls. Try on as many as possible. Look for wide shoulder straps, lumbar support, and a wide hip belt. Make sure it feels good and ask lots of questions. If your questions are not answered with painstaking detail so that you feel sure and secure, move on. One of the worst things possible for backcountry trips is an uncomfortable or poorly fitting pack.

Now for the fun stuff—packing everything you need to subsist inside this bag you've bought. One easy way: Pull everything out you want, then return most of it from whence it came. You really don't need three pair of pants or shorts, or 10 T-shirts. See the essential gear list that follows, reprinted from *Outside Magazine's Adventure Guide to Northern California*, by Andrew Rice.

As for food, a mix of dried food (pastas, lentils, beans, dried meats, and fruit), crackers, cereal, trail mix (try nuts, raisins, and M&M's), granola bars, envelopes of premade soups, and plastic jars of peanut butter and jelly work great. One guy I know hiked the Appalachian Trail with entire loaves of peanut butter and jelly sandwiches, all premade and repacked into the bread bag. It worked. And don't forget about water. There is plenty of water in Yosemite's high country, but you'll need to treat it to prevent *Giardia*. Don't take chances: This little bug is one painful parasite to ingest.

**Tuolumne Meadows to Agnew Meadows along the John Muir Trail.**
28 miles/3 days. Strenuous. The trailhead begins where the above hike ends, or take Hwy. 120 to Tuolumne Meadows and the signed trailhead parking area for the John Muir/Pacific Crest Trail/Lyell Fork hikes.

## Equipment Checklist

This list includes everything necessary for a trip of 2 or more days. It's more or less a backpackers' list for a 4- to 7-day summer-to-fall trip or a long-distance trail. This list can also be tailored for canoeing, backcountry skiing, etc.

*Kitchen:* lightweight water filter pump (Pur, First Need, Sweetwater Guardian); 2 or 3 Nalgene quart-size water bottles; 5-gallon camp water bag; stainless steel cook set; wooden spoon; backpacking stove (such as MSR Whisperlite or Coleman PEAK 1); 1¹/₂ to 2 quarts of stove fuel; kitchen matches; biodegradable soap; scouring pad; washcloth, pot holder, towel.

*Pantry:* coffee singles or tea bags; breakfast foods such as instant oatmeal; lunch items such as peanut butter and jelly, crackers, cheese, hard sausage; snacks such as gorp, beef jerky, dried fruits; dinners such as macaroni and cheese, freeze-dried dinners, couscous and Knorr gravy, other one-pot meals in Ziploc bags.

*Bedroom:* waterproof ground cloth; tent (3-season Moss, North Face, or Sierra Designs), sleeping bag rated to 20°F, sleeping pad (Therma-Rests are good).

*Clothes Closet:* boots, two pair heavy socks, polypropylene socks, polypropylene long johns, shorts or swimsuit, baseball cap or sun hat, knit wool cap, bandana, water/wind-resistant breathable shell, rain pants, cotton/synthetic T-shirt, fleece jacket, fleece pants, sport sandals, clothes sack.

*All-Purpose Essentials:* maps, compass, bug repellent, lighter, whistle (for bear country or rescue), sunglasses, watch, toothbrush,

A high-altitude climb that offers a weekend getaway that leaves flatlanders breathless, this hike offers some of the eastern Sierra's most pristine beauty. Be warned—it's a real heart-thumper. You'll trek through Donohue Pass at 11,056 feet. From the pass it's mostly downhill.

**Yosemite Creek.** 17 miles/1–2 days. Moderate to strenuous. Take Hwy. 120 east past the White Wolf Campground to the trailhead, which is just before a bridge sign for Yosemite Creek. The trailhead is on the south side of the highway.

This hike approaches the falls from behind and ends up at the same place as the Yosemite Falls hike described in chapter 3, without the steep climb up from the valley floor. After hiking 2 miles, you'll see razor, other toilet gear, miniflashlight or head lamp, extra batteries, battery-powered candle or lantern, Swiss army knife, 70 to 100 feet of rope or parachute cord for hanging food, etc., toilet paper, toilet trowel, extra quart-size Ziploc bags, extra gallon-size Ziploc bags, extra stuff sack, notebook and pen, a good book.

*First-Aid Kit:* 2-inch-by-3-inch moleskin, pair of small shears, thermometer, safety pins, ibuprofen, aspirin, acetaminophen, diarrhea pills, antacid tablets, sunscreen, sting-relief pads, iodine solution, iodine ointment, triple antibiotic ointment, antiseptic towelettes, single-edge razor blade or scalpel, 1-inch-by-3-inch fabric bandages, fabric knuckle bandages, sterile wound-closure strips (butterfly bandages), 4-inch-by-4-inch sterile gauze pads, adhesive tape, elastic bandage (Ace style), 5-inch-by-9-inch combine dressings, irrigation syringe, wire mesh splint.

*Luxuries:* GPS (global positioning system) device, camera gear, binoculars, fishing gear, flask (filled).

*Locations of Ranger Stations:* Outside the valley, there are three ranger stations and information centers. The Wawona Information Station (☎ **209/375-9501**) and Big Oak Flat Information Center (☎ **209/372-0615**) have general park information. The Tuolumne Meadows Visitor Center (☎ **209/372-0263**) has trail advice as well. The Valley Visitor Center (☎ **209/372-0299**) is the park's largest center, but you may have better luck contacting the Public Information Office at ☎ 209/372-0265. The Valley Wilderness Center also has maps, permits, and good advice.

the Yosemite Creek Campground. Hike through the campground to the Yosemite Falls Trail. In about 1.75 miles, you'll hit another junction. Head left and south and hike for another 4 miles to Upper Yosemite Fall. The view from here is heart-stopping. The valley looks like something out of Disneyland with its tiny lodges, people, and cars far below. The waterfall is surrounded by slick rock, so be careful, especially in wet conditions. Every year it seems someone slips over the edge into the abyss below. You can hike back the way you came, or head down the path to the valley if you've got a shuttle system set up or someone to take you back to your car. It's also possible in the summer months to take a bus from the valley to points along Highway 120. See the beginning of this chapter for more information.

**Yosemite Valley to Tuolumne Meadows along the John Muir Trail.**
22 miles/2 days. Moderate to strenuous. The trail begins in the valley at the Happy Isles parking area.

The trail is well marked and heads from the valley floor past Half Dome and then up to Cathedral Peak. Cathedral Lakes are nearby and worth a side trip. Camp at Tuolumne Meadows.

## SIDE TRIPS FROM HIGH SIERRA CAMPS

**Glen Aulin to Waterwheel Falls.** 7.6 miles/8 hours. Strenuous (but worth it). Cross Conness Creek and the trailhead is on your left about 30 feet ahead.

The walk is long and arduous but takes you to six major waterfalls along the Tuolumne. You'll climb about 1,000 feet along open ledges on the river. There's a lot to see, so get an early start. The trail switches along the noisy river, into a forest, and across a meadow. The most notable waterfalls begin about 1.5 miles into the hike and range from long, uninterrupted ribbons to 50-foot-long, 20-foot-wide masses of white water. The trail descends through a canyon. Watch for signs to Glen Aulin (about 3.5 miles away). You'll see LeConte Falls on your left beyond a few campsites. It cascades in broad, thin sheets of water, some stretching 30 feet wide as they flow down steeply sloping ledges along the river. A half-mile past LeConte is the top of Waterwheel Falls, a set of long, narrow falls that roar through a trough in the ledge to the left of the trail. With enough water and force, some of the water hits the ledge rock with sufficient force to propel it upward and back in a circle, like a pinwheel. Backward waterwheels are rare and should not be confused with the upward and forward spinning of water of LeConte Falls. You can climb down to Waterwheel Falls—it'll add a steep half-mile to your trip—before returning to Glen Aulin.

**Sunrise High Sierra Camp to Upper Cathedral Lake.** 10 miles/6–8 hours. Moderate to strenuous. The hike begins next to the dining tent.

Descend the stone steps to the John Muir Trail along the north side of a meadow. The trail skirts a meadow and crosses several small creeks. Stick to the John Muir Trail, which will bring you to a branch of Cathedral Fork, which has a bed lined with rust-colored rocks. After 2 miles, the trail falls away from the creek and toward Columbia Finger, climbing a rocky slope that quickly levels off. You'll see a variety of peaks along the way, and toward the end, when Cathedral Peak comes into view, you'll be surrounded by

2-mile-high pinnacles that somehow escaped the prehistoric glaciers. The trail descends through a meadow, then on to Upper Cathedral Lake. The trek back to camp offers stunning views from the reverse perspective.

**Vogelsang High Sierra Camp to Vogelsang Pass.** 3 miles/2–3 hours. Moderate to strenuous. The walk begins on the west side of the dining tent and descends to Fletcher Creek.

Turn left and walk 50 feet upstream and cross the creek. Views will appear quickly. The twin towers of Vogelsang Peak lie ahead, stretched apart like some enormous saddle. This walk also offers views of Vogelsang Lake. The rough slopes of Vogelsang Peak on the right and Vogelsang Pass are straight ahead. A 50-foot-wide pond surrounded by pinkish granite marks the top of the pass. Cross to the north side for one of the most spectacular views in the High Sierra. Walk a few feet more, to where the trail descends toward Lewis Creek, to see a panoramic sight: 12,080-foot Parson's Peak, 12,503-foot Simmons Peak, 12,960-foot Mt. Maclure, the wide 12,561-foot Mt. Florence, the summits of Clark Range, Triple Divide and Merced peaks, the aptly named Red and Gray peaks, and Mt. Clark. Look down and you'll see the blue-green Bernice Lake.

# 5

# Where to Stay & Eat in Yosemite

*T*here are accommodations to fit every budget and every taste in or near Yosemite. The valley itself caters to families and offers everything from campgrounds to the opulent Ahwahnee Hotel where every room has a view on the sheer granite greatness of the valley. Parking is available at or near each site within the valley. All sites are located at or near shuttle bus stops.

A more narrow scope of choices is available outside the valley but still within the park, at Wawona, Tuolumne Meadows, White Wolf, and a host of other campsites, as well as privately owned cabins and bed-and-breakfast accommodations. In addition, there are accommodations and campgrounds in and near the towns that serve as gateways to the park. Note that prices are subject to change without notice.

## 1 Lodging

### INSIDE THE PARK

Lodging in the park is under the auspices of Yosemite Concession Services Corp. Rooms can be reserved up to 366 days in advance (☎ 209/252-4848). Reservations are also accepted by mail at Yosemite Reservations, 5410 E. Howe Ave., Fresno, CA 93727.

The exception to all of this is Wawona. While YCS operates the Wawona Hotel, there are several dozen private homes that are rented seasonally through Redwood Guest Cottages. It's a real hodgepodge and appears fairly hit-and-miss in terms of quality, which may be why these places are seldom mentioned in guidebooks. But it's an option (☎ 209/375-6666).

**The Ahwahnee.** Yosemite Valley. ☎ **209/252-4848.** 95 rms, 4 suites, 24 cottages. A/C TEL. $229.50 for all regular rms and cottages; up to $485 for suites. Lower rates Dec–Jan. CB, DC, DISC, JCB, MC, V. Rates include coffee and pastries for breakfast. Parking available or take the shuttle bus to stop No. 4.

The hotel's accommodations are fit for a king or queen, and it has hosted both. Queen Elizabeth slept here, as did President

John F. Kennedy, actor Clint Eastwood, poet Alfred Noyes, and quarterback Steve Young. It's tough to top The Ahwahnee, a six-story rock structure that offers beautiful views from every window. The hotel has a number of common rooms on the ground floor. There are three fireplaces large enough to stand in, and the rooms are furnished with large overstuffed sofas and chairs on which to read or play games. Guest rooms are upstairs, with suites located on the top floor, accessible only by special elevator key. Suites include a pair of rooms: one for sleeping and another for sitting. The Sun Suite is a bright pair of rooms in lime and yellow with comfy lounges and floor-to-ceiling French windows that open out onto the valley. The library room's rich decor includes a fireplace and walls of books. Regular rooms offer a choice of two double or one king-size bed, with a couch and plush towels and snuggly comforters. Rooms have original stencils on the walls dating back to 1927, when the hotel was built. The entire hotel received a $1.5 million renovation in January 1997.

**Dining/Entertainment:** The Ahwahnee offers a fine selection of food, most notably in its spacious dining room (see "Where to Eat," later in this chapter). Breakfast is served from 7 to 10:30am, lunch from 11:30am to 3pm, and dinner from 5 to 9:30pm. Prices vary depending on the meal, but be forewarned—it's expensive, but the food is excellent. Reservations are necessary for dinner (☎ 209/372-1489). The hotel also has a lounge with a full bar and limited food service.

**Services:** Dry cleaning, laundry service, newspaper delivery, nightly turndown, baby-sitting for children out of diapers, express checkout, valet parking.

**Facilities:** VCRs available upon request, Primestar movie channel, outdoor pool, sundecks, nature trails, conference rooms, tour desk, boutiques.

**Curry Village.** Yosemite Valley. ☎ **209/252-4848.** 427 canvas tent-cabins with central shared bath and about 100 wooden cabins, some with bath. Reservations suggested. $42 per tent-cabin, double occupancy, with additional charge for extra adults or children. Cabin $59.25–$75.25 with bath, double occupancy, with an additional charge for extra adults. Lower rates Nov–Mar. CB, DC, DISC, JCB, MC, V. Parking is available or take the shuttle bus to stop Nos. 1, 13, and 14.

Curry Village is a mass of white canvas tents that dot the valley's south slope. It was founded in 1899 as a cheaper alternative for valley visitors at a mere $2 a day, but guests can kiss those days goodbye. Today, it's often condemned as a kiddie hell hole, filled in the summer with crying and roughhousing. We found it tolerable and the easiest place to crash. It is also home to a decent pizza parlor with beer by the pitcher and a large-screen TV, a hamburger shack, a general store with the valley's best wine selection (still meager), one grossly overpriced cafeteria, and an ice-cream stand. It has a main tour desk where guests can book events throughout the valley. Canvas tents have wood floors, sleep two to four people, and are equipped with beds, dressers, and an ample supply of wool blankets. Tents have electrical outlets and daily maid service. In short, convenience usually makes this worth the noisy toddler next door.

**Dining/Entertainment:** Hamburger stand, ice-cream stand, cafeteria, pizza parlor with big-screen TV, mountaineering school, sports shop.

**Facilities:** Outdoor swimming pool, sundeck, bicycle rentals, raft rentals, nature trails, children's programs, tour desk.

**Housekeeping Camp.** Yosemite Valley. ☎ 209/252-4848. 266 units, all with shared rest rooms and shower facilities. Reservations required. $44.50 per site (up to 4 people; $4 for every extra person). Shower house. CB, DC, DISC, JCB, MC, V. Open summer only.

This place is funky. It's the closest thing to camping without pitching a tent. The sites are fence-enclosed shanties built on concrete slabs, each with a table, cupboard, electrical outlets, shelves, a mirror, and lights. The sleeping areas have two single-size fold-down bunks and a double bed. The park is slowly eliminating sites at Housekeeping Camp, with the idea of eventually getting the number of units down to 232.

**Facilities:** Nature trails, Laundromat.

559

**Tuolumne Meadows Lodge.** Hwy. 120, Tuolumne Meadows, Yosemite National Park. ☎ 209/252-4848. 69 canvas tent-cabins, all with shared bath and shower house. $44 double, with additional $7.50 per adult or $3.50 per child. CB, DC, DISC, JCB, MC, V. Parking available in an adjacent lot. Closed in winter. From Yosemite Valley, take Hwy. 120 east 55 miles toward Tioga Pass.

Not a lodge, but another group of canvas tent-cabins. Like White Wolf, these also have wood-burning stoves, tables, and sleep up to four. The crowds get thicker here as this is prime hiking territory. Not only do hikes begin here, this is home base for wilderness trekkers and backcountry campers. There's also a tiny general store and restaurant.

**Facilities:** Nature trails, tour desk.

**Wawona Hotel.** Hwy. 41, Wawona, Yosemite National Park. ☎ 209/252-4848. 104 rms, 50 with shared bath. $70.75–$97.50 double, with additional charge for extra adults. CB, DC, DISC, JCB, MC, V. From Yosemite Valley, take Hwy. 41 south 27 miles toward Fresno.

This is a classic Victorian-style hotel comprised of six stately white buildings set near towering trees in a green clearing. Don't be surprised if a horse and buggy round the driveway by the fishpond—it's that kind of place. Maybe it's the wide porches, the nearby 9-hole golf course, or the vines of hops cascading from one veranda to the next. The entire place was designated a National Historic Landmark in 1987. Clark Cottage is the oldest building, dating back to 1876. The main hotel was built in 1879. Rooms are comfortable and quaint with a choice of a double and a twin, a king, or a double bed (most of the latter share baths). All rooms open onto wide porches and overlook green lawns. Clark Cottage is the most intimate. The main hotel has the widest porches and plenty of Adirondack chairs, and at night the downstairs sun room hosts a pianist. Check out the whistling maintenance man who hits every high note in the "Star Spangled Banner" while the American flag is hoisted each morning (leaving many bystanders speechless as more than a few Wawona employees chime to complete this whistling orchestra).

**Dining/Entertainment:** An adjacent dining room serves great food and an awesome Sunday brunch. Breakfast is served daily from 7:30 to 10am, a lunch buffet is from noon to 1:30pm, dinner is 5:30 to 8:30pm (until 9pm on Friday and Saturday), and Sunday brunch is 7:30am to 1:30pm. There is also a lounge.

**Facilities:** Large outdoor pool, sundecks, two outdoor tennis courts, golf course, nature trails, conference rooms.

**White Wolf Lodge.** Hwy. 120, White Wolf, Yosemite National Park. ☎ **209/ 252-4848.** 24 canvas tent-cabins, 4 cabins. All canvas cabins share bath and shower house. $44–$80 double, with an additional charge of $7.50 per adult and $3.50 per child. CB, DC, DISC, JCB, MC, V. Parking available across a 2-lane road. Closed in winter. From Yosemite Valley, take Hwy. 120 east 33 miles toward Tioga Pass.

Imagine a smaller, quieter, cleaner Curry Village with larger tents, each equipped with a wood-burning stove. This small outpost was bypassed when Tioga Road was rebuilt. White Wolf Lodge is not a lodge but a cluster of canvas tent-cabins, a few wooden ones out front, and a general store/restaurant. It's located halfway between the valley and the high country, and generally isn't overrun with visitors. It's a popular spot for midweek hikers and weekend stopovers. It can get crowded but retains a homey feeling. Maybe it's the fact that there's no electricity after 11pm when the generator shuts off. Wood cabins all have a private bath and resemble a regular motel room, with neat little porches and chairs out front. Canvas cabins beat the Curry Village style by a mile. Each sleeps four in any combination of twin and double beds. There's a table and the helpful staff will show guests how to work the wood-burning stove. Benches outside give guests someplace to rest their weary feet and watch the stars. Bathrooms are clean and access is controlled by guests, with the exception of a few midday hours when nearby campers can pay for showers.

**Facilities:** Nature trails.

**Yosemite Lodge.** Yosemite Valley. ☎ **209/252-4848.** 249 motel rms and suites. Reservations suggested. Some with A/C. $70.50–$107.25 double occupancy, with additional charge for extra adults. Lower rates Nov–Mar. CB, DC, DISC, JCB, MC, V. Parking available or take the shuttle bus to stop No. 8.

This is a conglomerate of cabins, regular motel rooms, and suites. Most rooms offer one or two double or king-size beds. They are unremarkable but comfortable and clean. Some look out on Yosemite Falls, and some have patios or terraces. It's not uncommon to see deer and other wildlife scamper through this area. Spring mornings offer a wonderful orchestra of songbirds and some stunning views of Yosemite Falls at sunrise.

**Dining:** The complex also contains an overpriced cafeteria, the new Mountain Room Restaurant, which has great views and wonderful desserts, and the Garden Terrace, which serves an awesome salad bar. There is also a lounge, general store, and tour desk where guests can book events throughout the valley.

**Services:** Baby-sitting.

**Facilities:** Large outdoor swimming pool, sundeck, bicycle rentals, nature trails, children's programs, conference rooms, tour desk.

**Yosemite West Cottages.** P.O. Box 36, Yosemite National Park. ☎ **209/642-2211.** A fluctuating number of cabins and private homes. TV. $85–$150 and up. Take Hwy. 41 for 12 miles north of Wawona.

Yosemite West rents private homes and cottages in the park that range in size and accommodate families as well as couples. All cabins have kitchenettes, and the vacation homes have full kitchens. It's just like living in the park. Homes are equipped with oversize beds and are ready and warm upon arrival. From here it's 10 miles to the valley and 8 miles to Badger Pass.

## OUTSIDE THE PARK

If you strike out in the park, or prefer to stay outside, there is a plethora of choices. Each gateway community has built up a strong tourist trade catering to travelers.

## ALONG HIGHWAY 120 (EASTBOUND)

**Groveland Hotel.** 18767 Hwy. 120, Groveland. ☎ **800/273-3314** or 209/
962-4000. Fax 209/962-6674. 17 rms, including 3 suites. All with private bath,
4 with shower only. A/C TEL. $95–$175 double, $25 for each extra person. Rates
include continental breakfast and wine in the evening. AE, CB, DC, DISC, MC, V.

This is a great place to stay. The rooms are spacious, the hosts are
gracious, and there's enough history, good food, and conversation
to give travelers pause before heading into Yosemite. Groveland is
about as quaint a town as you can get, and Peggy and Grover Mosley
have poured their heart into making their hotel an elegant but comfortable place to stay. Vacant for years and on the verge of tumbling
down, the Mosleys decided to forgo a quiet retirement from very
interesting careers (you'll have to ask for yourself) to renovate and
reopen the hotel. It is now a historic landmark. The hotel was built
in 1849 to house workers constructing the nearby Hetch Hetchy
Dam. Most of the rooms are upstairs and many have large spa bathtubs. Most rooms are named after women of the Sierra. One exception is Lyle's Room, named for the hotel's resident ghost. Return
patrons swear it's true. Lyle's disdain for clutter atop one bureau was
vouched for by a patron who swears her makeup case was moved to
the sink. Then there's Charlie's Room, named for a hard-driving,
tobacco-spitting resident who drove a stagecoach, then started a
trucking company. When he died, the townspeople learned he was
a she. All rooms are filled with antiques, have thick down comforters, beds you want to jump on, and plush robes. Suites have fireplaces. The Mosleys' attention to detail is what makes the Groveland
Hotel a super spot. No wonder it was picked as one of the nation's
top 10 inns in 1997 by *Country Inns* magazine.

**Dining/Entertainment:** The hotel also has a great dining room.
Small, candlelit, and the best food in town—also the most expensive. The food is tasty (see "Where to Eat," later in this chapter) and
the wine list is fantastic. Wine is one of Peggy Mosley's passions.
Reservations are not necessary but are suggested in summer. Dinner
is served from 6 to 11pm in summer and 6 to 8:30pm in winter.
Attire is casual.

**Services:** Room service, safe on premises.

**Facilities:** Conference rooms, 18-hole golf course 5 miles away.

**Hotel Charlotte.** 18736 Hwy. 120, Groveland. ☎ **800/961-7799** or 209/
962-6455. 11 rms, 3 with shared bath, 2 with shower only. A/C in summer only.
$56.70–$124.20 double. Rates include continental breakfast. AE, MC, V.

Walking into the Charlotte is like stepping back in time. Built in 1918
by an Italian immigrant of the same name, it's warm, comfortable,

and no-nonsense. You'll be greeted in the lobby filled with antiques and red velvet–covered furnishings. The rooms are all upstairs. The hotel offers twin, double, and queen beds. Several rooms adjoin each other and have connecting bathrooms (perfect for families). Rooms are quaint and have the basics but nothing more. There is also a common game-television room. The continental breakfast is great—strong coffee, fresh warm muffins, and juices.

**Dining:** Casual dining is offered downstairs from 6 to 10pm in summer and 6 to 9pm in winter. Reservations are not necessary but may help speed things up during the summer.

**Facilities:** 18-hole golf course 5 miles away.

**Inn at Sugar Pine Ranch.** 21250 Hwy. 120, Groveland. ☎ **888/800-7823** or 209/962-7823. 12 rms and cottages. All with private bath, 8 with shower only. A/C. $110–$150 double, $25 for each extra person. Rates include full breakfast. MC, V.

This whitewashed inn is a new addition along the route to Yosemite, but its buildings date back to the turn of the century and beyond. It's just outside of Groveland headed toward the park. The main building is an old farmhouse built in 1860. There are also separate cottages. Everything is laid out beneath tall pine trees. Rooms are comfortable and plush. Some cottages have whirlpool bathtubs and fireplaces. Some rooms have balconies. All have nice views.

**Facilities:** Outdoor pool, nature trails, 7 miles to 18-hole golf course.

## ALONG HIGHWAY 140

**Best Western Yosemite Way Station.** 4999 Hwy. 140, Mariposa. ☎ **800/528-1234** or 209/966-7545. Fax 209/966-6353. 76 rms. A/C TV TEL. $79–$85 double, $6 for each additional person. Rates include continental breakfast. AE, CB, DC, DISC, MC, V.

Typical motel accommodations. Clean and comfortable, but nothing fancy. It is within walking distance of restaurants and shops and is near public transportation to Yosemite.

**Facilities:** Pool, Jacuzzi, conference room.

**Cedar Lodge.** 9966 Hwy. 140, El Portal. ☎ **800/321-5261** or 209/379-2612. Fax 209/379-2712. 206 rms, some family units, 1 three-bedroom suite with private pool and Jacuzzi. A/C TV TEL. $85–$125 double; $275–$375 suite. AE, MC, V.

Eight miles outside the park, this lodge offers ample-size rooms in a wooded setting. It is owned by Yosemite Motels, which operates six motels outside the park. Variety makes this place an attractive option for visitors. It can accommodate every size group, from couples to families and large groups. Conference room seating is available for 250. There are two restaurants and a lounge on the premises. Public buses to the park are available from here.

**Facilities:** Kitchenettes, VCRs, video rentals, indoor and outdoor pools, Jacuzzi, conference rooms.

**Comfort Inn.** 4994 Bullion St., Mariposa. ☎ **800/321-5261** or 209/966-4344. Fax 209/966-4655. 78 rms, suites with full kitchens. A/C TV TEL. $79–$85 double; $180–$350 suite. Rates include continental breakfast. AE, CB, DC, DISC, MC, V.

Regular motel-style accommodations. Large, clean rooms and conveniently located within walking distance of restaurants and near public transportation to Yosemite.

**Facilities:** Pool, Jacuzzi.

**Mariposa Hotel-Inn.** 5029 Hwy. 140, Mariposa. ☎ **800/317-3244** or 209/966-4676. Fax 209/742-5963. 5 rms. A/C TV. $75–$89 double, $10 for each additional person. Rates include continental breakfast. Rates 15% lower Nov–Mar. AE, DISC, MC, V.

A former stage stop, this building was converted to a hotel in 1901. It has undergone several renovations since, each in an effort to expand the size of its rooms. The charm of this historic building has been preserved. Guests enter from a large oak door at street level and climb an interior flight of stairs to the foyer, from which a long hall leads to individual rooms. All the rooms are large with sitting areas. The Marguerite Room has the hotel's original clawfoot bathtub. Della's Room is named after a Native American whose hand-woven baskets hang on the walls. Check out Nana's Room, a bright, well-lit room that gets the morning sun. The veranda at the rear of the hotel often serves as a gathering point for patrons to meet or eat breakfast. The hotel is close to shopping and restaurants.

**Miners Inn.** 5181 Hwy. 49 N., Mariposa. ☎ **800/321-5261** or 209/742-7777. Fax 209/742-4655. 76 rms. A/C TV TEL. $75–$159 double, $6 for each additional person. AE, DC, DISC, MC, V.

A standard motel in a rustic setting that strives to recapture the Old West. Deluxe rooms include spa tubs and fireplaces. There is an on-site restaurant and lounge, and there's nearby public transportation to Yosemite.

**Facilities:** Pool, Jacuzzi, kitchenettes.

**Mother Lode Lodge.** 5052 Hwy. 140, Mariposa. ☎ **800/398-9770** or 209/966-2521. 14 rms, including a suite and family unit. TV. $39–$65 double. Lower rates in off-season. Rates include continental breakfast in summer. DISC, MC, V.

Best on the budget. The no-frills rooms here are sparse but clean. Basic rooms have one or two queen-size beds, a small desk, and a mirror. The bathrooms are tiny and the televisions have very few channels.

**Facilities:** Outdoor pool.

**Poppy Hill Bed & Breakfast.** 5218 Crystal Aire Dr., Mariposa. ☎ **800/58-POPPY** or 209/742-6273. 3 rms, 2 with shared bath. A/C. $85–$100 double Apr–Sept, $75–$90 Oct–Mar. $20 each additional person. Rates include full breakfast. AE, CB, DC, DISC, MC, V. Take Hwy. 140 past Mariposa 3 miles, turn left on Whitlock Rd. and right on Crystal Aire Dr.

This restored country home filled with antiques offers queen-size beds, down comforters, bathrobes, sitting areas, and scenic views.

**Facilities:** Aboveground pool and Jacuzzi.

**Yosemite View Lodge.** 11156 Hwy. 140, El Portal. ☎ **800/321-5261** or 209/379-2681. Fax 209/379-2704. 158 rms with kitchenettes. A/C TV TEL. $129–$169 double. MC, V.

Just outside Arch Rock entrance, this lodge offers guests accommodations on the river, which can turn wet and wild during the spring. All rooms have refrigerators and microwaves; some have spa tubs and fireplaces. A new restaurant is under construction. Public buses to the park are available.

**Facilities:** Kitchenettes, two outdoor pools, three outdoor Jacuzzis.

## ALONG HIGHWAY 41

**Comfort Inn.** 40489 Hwy. 41, Oakhurst. ☎ **800/321-5261** or 209/683-8282. Fax 209/658-7030. 113 rms, 2 suites. A/C TV TEL. $80–$120 double. Lower rates off-season. Rates include continental breakfast. AE, CB, DC, DISC, MC, V.

This place offers regular motel-style accommodations and large, clean rooms. It's one of the larger motels outside the park that may have that last-minute room you need.

**Facilities:** Pool, Jacuzzi, near the River Creek and Ahwahnee golf courses.

**Ducey's on the Lake.** Pines Village, N. Shore, Bass Lake, P.O. Box 109, Bass Lake. ☎ **800/350-7463** or 209/642-3902. 20 rms and suites. A/C TV. $168–$298 double in summer, $105–$210 in winter; $300–$350 suite. CB, DC, DISC, JCB, MC, V. From Hwy. 41, take Rd. 222 to the north shore of Bass Lake.

This historic country inn offers a variety of leisure activities. Guests stay in chalets and rooms that boast Native American decor and comfortable furnishings. Vaulted ceilings and beams were built with trees from the 44-acre property. Large bathrooms have plush towels and thick bathrobes. All units have terraces and fireplaces, and some have whirlpools.

**Dining/Entertainment:** Three restaurants, bar, baby-sitting, twice daily maid service.

**Facilities:** VCRs, movie channels, sundeck, tennis courts, jogging track, nature trails, conference rooms, laundry.

**Oakhurst Lodge.** 40302 Hwy. 41, Oakhurst. ☎ **800/655-6343** or 209/683-4417. Fax 209/683-4417, ext. 171. 60 rms. A/C TV TEL. $57–$63 double. Lower rates off-season. AE, CB, DC, DISC, MC, V.

This place offers clean rooms with one or two queen-size beds. There's a good selection of cable television channels and all rooms have small refrigerators. The motel is within walking distance of numerous restaurants and adjacent to a nice picnic area.

**Facilities:** Outdoor pool. Near the River Creek and Ahwahnee golf courses.

**Rose Pine Inn.** 41703 Rd. 222, Oakhurst. ☎ **209/642-2800.** 9 rms, 7 with full bath, one with shower only. A/C TV. $55–$95 in summer, cheaper in winter. Rates include expanded continental breakfast. MC, V. Take Hwy. 41 through Oakhurst 3 miles to Rd. 222, turn right, and drive exactly 2 miles. The inn is on your left.

Rooms range from single bedrooms to split-level family cottages nestled in a picturesque canyon. The Garden Room is pretty, with a separate entrance, private bath, kitchenette, and nice porch. The family units are spacious. One includes a deep bathtub, slate tile, nice patio, living room, and full kitchen. The Hidden Rose Room is small but romantic, with a spa perfect for a massage while relaxing in front of the television. The owners are helpful and unobtrusive and guests benefit from the Rose Pine Inn's off-the-beaten-path location—the accommodations are a bargain. The homemade cinnamon rolls for breakfast are yummy.

**Facilities:** Near the River Creek and Ahwahnee golf courses.

**Tenaya Lodge.** 1122 Hwy. 41, Fish Camp. ☎ **800/635-5807** or 209/683-6555. Fax 209/683-8684. 244 rms, 20 suites. A/C MINIBAR TV TEL. $159–$239 double in summer, $69–$209 in winter. Add $20–$80 for suites. Buffet breakfast $11 per couple. Children stay free in parents' rm. AE, DC, DISC, JCB, MC, V.

Whoever built this place had one foot in the Adirondack Mountains and another in the Southwest. This three- and four-story resort opened in 1990 on 35 acres full of hiking trails. The rest of the lodge includes a gas station and general store. The lobby has an impressive fireplace towering three stories and built of river rock. The staff is nice, helpful, and accommodating. The rooms are ultramodern with multiple phones and a built-in safe.

**Dining/Entertainment:** Three restaurants, which comprise all after-hours activity between Oakhurst and Yosemite.

**Services:** Room service.

**Facilities:** Indoor and outdoor swimming pools, on-site massage specialists, health club, game room, sleigh and hay rides depending on season.

## 2 Camping

Campsite reservations in Yosemite are accepted in 1-month blocks beginning on the 15th of each month and can be made up to 3 months in advance. That said, make your reservations as soon following the 15th of the month, 3 months in advance, as you can, especially for sites in the valley. Additional campground information is available by Touch-Tone phone at ☎ **209/372-0200.**

As this book went to press, the National Park Service had just selected a new company to handle their camping reservations for parks across the country. Biospherics, Inc., a Maryland-based company, is expected to be up and running by March 15, 1998. To make a reservation to camp in Yosemite National Park, call ☎ **800/436-7275.** If you are unsuccessful using this number, try the general Yosemite information line at ☎ **209/372-0200.**

*Note:* Wilderness permits are required for all overnight backpacking trips in the park. No wilderness camping is allowed in the valley. For more information on wilderness camping, including Yosemite's High Sierra camps, see chapter 4.

In Yosemite National Park there is a 7-day camping limit in the valley and Wawona, and a 14-day limit elsewhere, from May 1 to September 15. For the remaining months of the year, there is a 30-day limit. Some campgrounds are closed in winter, so call in advance. Some sites are first-come, first-served. A maximum of six people and two vehicles may stay at each campsite. Checkout time is noon. Pets are allowed in some campgrounds.

Now for the bad news: The valley lost half of its roughly 800 campsites during a flood in early 1997. The lost campsites will eventually be replaced further away from the Merced River, but no one's predicting when construction will begin.

Outside the park, campgrounds range from $9 to $11 per night in national forests, and are first-come, first-served. Private campgrounds are also available.

## INSIDE THE PARK

**Bridalveil Creek.** Glacier Point, Yosemite National Park. ☎ **209/372-0200** for recorded information. 110 tent and RV sites. 1 group campsite. No reservations. $10. Piped water. Flush toilets, fireplaces, and picnic tables. Pets permitted. The campground can also accommodate some pack animals; call for information. Open June–Oct. Take Hwy. 41 (from either direction) to Glacier Point Rd. The campground is about 8 miles down the road.

Near the beautiful Glacier Point, this first-come, first-served campground is away from the valley crowds but within a moderate drive to the valley sights. The campground is set along Bridalveil Creek, which flows to Bridalveil Fall, a beauty of a waterfall, especially after a heavy winter or wet spring.

**Crane Flat.** Big Oak Flat Entrance, Yosemite National Park. ☎ **800/436-7275.** 166 tent and RV sites. $15. Piped water. Flush toilets, fireplaces, and picnic tables. Pets permitted. A grocery, gas station, and propane gas are nearby. Evening ranger programs. Open June–Oct. From Buck Meadows, drive 20 miles east on Hwy. 120 to the campground.

Near the Big Trees and away from valley crowds, this is a large but nice campground with the essential comforts nearby. Yosemite Valley is about 20 miles away.

**Hodgdon Meadow.** Big Oak Flat Entrance, Yosemite National Park. ☎ **800/436-7275.** 105 tent and RV sites, including some group and walk-in sites. Reservations required May–Sept. $15. Piped water. Flush toilets, fireplaces, and picnic tables. A grocery store and propane gas are nearby. Pets permitted. From Buck Meadows, drive 13 miles east on Hwy. 120 to the campground.

Yosemite Valley is 25 miles away; the Big Trees are 3 miles southeast. The campground is located along North Crane Creek and near the Tuolumne River's south fork.

**Lower Pines.** Yosemite Valley. ☎ **800/436-7275.** 60 tent and RV sites. $15. Piped water. Flush toilets, fireplaces, and picnic tables. Showers can be bought nearby at Camp Curry for about $2. A grocery, laundry, propane gas, rafting, bicycle and ski rentals are nearby. Open Mar–Oct. Parking is available or take the shuttle bus to stop No. 19.

Like most campgrounds in Yosemite Valley, Lower Pines is wide open with lots of shade but limited privacy. Still, it's a nice place. Easy to camp. Clean bathrooms. Bordered on the north by a nice meadow.

**North Pines, Yosemite Valley.** ☎ **800/436-7275.** 85 tent and RV sites. $15. Piped water. Flush toilets, fireplaces, and picnic tables. Showers can be bought nearby at Camp Curry for about $2. A grocery, laundry, propane gas, rafting, bicycle and ski rentals are nearby. Open Apr–Oct. Parking is available, or take the shuttle bus to stop No. 18.

## Yosemite Campgrounds

| Campground | Elev. (ft.) | Total Sites | RV Hook-ups | Dump Station | Toilets | Drinking Water | Showers | Fire Pits/Grills | Laundry | Public Phone | Reservations Possible | Fees | Open |
|---|---|---|---|---|---|---|---|---|---|---|---|---|---|
| **Inside Yosemite National Park** | | | | | | | | | | | | | |
| Bridalveil Creek | 7,200 | 110 | 0 | no | yes | yes | no | yes | no | yes | no | $10 | June–Oct |
| Crane Flat | 6,200 | 116 | 0 | no | yes | yes | no | yes | no | yes | yes | $15 | June–Oct |
| Hodgdon Meadow | 4,900 | 195 | 0 | no | yes | yes | no | yes | no | yes | May–Sept | $15 | all year |
| Lower Pines | 4,000 | 60 | 0 | nearby | yes | yes | nearby | yes | nearby | yes | yes | $15 | Mar–Oct |
| North Pines | 4,000 | 85 | 0 | nearby | yes | yes | nearby | yes | nearby | yes | yes | $15 | Apr–Oct |
| Porcupine Flat | 8,100 | 52 | 0 | no | yes | no | no | yes | no | yes | no | $6 | July–Sept |
| Sunnyside | 4,000 | 35 (tent only) | 0 | no | yes | yes | nearby | yes | nearby | yes | no | $3 | all year |
| Tamarack Flat | 6,200 | 52 (tent only) | 0 | no | yes | no | no | yes | no | yes | no | $6 | July–Sept |
| Tuolumne Meadows | 8,600 | 314 | 0 | nearby | yes | yes | nearby | yes | nearby | yes | for 1/2 the spaces | $6 | June–Sept |
| Upper Pines | 4,000 | 238 | 0 | yes | yes | yes | nearby | yes | no | yes | May–Sept | $15 | all year |
| Wawona | 4,000 | 100 | 0 | nearby | yes | yes | no | yes | no | yes | May–Sept | $15 | all year |
| White Wolf | 7,900 | 100 | 0 | no | yes | yes | nearby | yes | no | yes | no | $10 | July–Sept |
| Yosemite Creek | 6,200 | 75 (tent only) | 0 | no | yes | no | no | yes | no | yes | no | $6 | July–Sept |

| Outside the Park | | | | | | | | | | | | |
|---|---|---|---|---|---|---|---|---|---|---|---|---|
| Lumsden | 1,500 | 10 (tent only) | 0 | no | yes | no | no | yes | no | yes | free | Apr–Oct |
| Lumsden Bridge | 1,500 | 9 (tent only) | 0 | no | yes | no | no | yes | no | yes | free | Apr–Oct |
| Lost Claim | 3,100 | 10 | 0 | no | yes | hand-pumped | no | yes | no | yes | $8 | May–Oct |
| The Pines | 3,200 | 21 | 0 | no | yes | only to October | no | yes | no | yes | $9 | all year |
| South Fork | 1,500 | 25 | 0 | no | yes | no | no | yes | no | yes | free | Apr–Nov |
| Indian Flat | 1,500 | 35 | 0 | no | yes | yes | no | yes | no | yes | $9 | all year |
| Jerseydale | 5,800 | 12 | 0 | no | yes | yes | no | yes | no | yes | free | May–Nov |
| Summerdale | 5,000 | 30 | 0 | no | yes | yes | no | yes | no | yes | $9 | May–Oct |
| Summit Camp | 5,800 | 2 (tent) | 0 | no | yes | yes | no | yes | no | yes | free | June–Nov |
| Aspen Grove | 8,000 | 58 | 0 | no | yes | no | no | yes | no | yes | $5 | May–Oct |
| Big Bend | 7,800 | 18 | 0 | no | yes | yes | no | yes | no | yes | $7 | May–Oct |
| Ellery Lake | 9,500 | 13 | 0 | no | yes | yes | no | yes | no | yes | $7 | June–Oct |
| Junction | 9,600 | 10 | 0 | no | yes | no | no | yes | no | yes | free | June–Oct |
| Lee Vining | 8,000 | 129 | 0 | no | yes | no | no | yes | no | yes | $5 | May–Oct |
| Saddlebag Lake | 10,000 | 22 | 0 | no | yes | yes | no | yes | no | yes | $7 | May–Oct |
| Tioga Lake | 9,700 | 13 | 0 | no | yes | yes | no | yes | no | yes | $7 | June–Oct |
| Yosemite–Mariposa | 2,000 | 40 | 30 | yes | yes | yes | yes | yes | yes | yes | $18–$30 | all year |

Beautifully situated beneath a grove of pines trees that offer little privacy but big shade. It's also near the river and roughly a mile from Mirror Lake.

**Porcupine Flat.** White Wolf, Yosemite National Park. ☎ **209/372-0200** for recorded information. 52 tent and RV sites. No reservations. $6. No piped water. Pit toilets, fireplaces, and picnic tables. Open July–Sept. From Tuolumne Meadows, drive 16 miles west on Hwy. 120. From Yosemite Valley, drive 38 miles east on Hwy. 120.

Near Yosemite Creek, this is another great campground that may have space if you're in a pinch. It's first-come, first served, with lots of shade, shrubs, and trees.

**Sunnyside Walk-in.** Yosemite Valley. 35 tent sites. No reservations. $3 per person. Piped water. Flush toilets. Showers can be bought nearby at Camp Curry for about $2. Parking is available about 50 yards away or take the shuttle bus to stop No. 7.

This small campground is the most bohemian gathering in the valley, a magnet for hikers and climbers taking off or just returning from trips. It's situated behind Yosemite Lodge, near the trailhead for Yosemite Falls and near rocks frequently used by beginning rock climbers.

**Tamarack Flat.** Big Oak Flat Entrance, Yosemite National Park. ☎ **209/372-0200** for recorded information. 52 tent sites. No reservations. $6. No piped water. Pit toilets, fireplaces, and picnic tables. Open July–Sept. From Buck Meadows drive 21 miles east on Hwy. 120, bear left, and drive 3 miles to the campground entrance on the right. The campground is another 2.5 miles down the road.

Sort of off the beaten path, this little-known campground accessible by car is more secluded than most, which means fewer folks rest their heads here. It's equidistant from the valley and Tuolumne Meadows.

**Tuolumne Meadows Campground.** Tuolumne Meadows, Yosemite National Park. ☎ **800/436-7275.** 314 tent and RV sites. Reservations required for half the spaces. $15. Piped water. Flush toilets, fireplaces, picnic tables, and a dump station. Showers can be bought nearby at Tuolumne Lodge for a fee. Pets permitted. A grocery store is nearby. Open June–Sept. From Yosemite Valley, drive 46 miles east on Hwy. 120.

The biggest campground in Yosemite, and, amazingly, often the least crowded, this site in the high country makes a good spot from which to head off with a backpack. It's also near the Tuolumne River, hence good for fishing. The campground also has 25 walk-in spaces for backpackers and eight group sites that can accommodate up to 30 people each.

**Upper Pines.** Yosemite Valley. ☎ **800/436-7275.** 238 tent and RV sites. $15. Piped water. Flush toilets, fireplaces, picnic tables, and disposal station. Showers can be bought nearby at Camp Curry for about $2. A grocery, laundry, propane gas, rafting, bicycle and ski rentals are nearby. Pets permitted. Parking is available or take the shuttle bus to stop No. 15 or 19.

The only valley campground that allows pets and the valley's only campground open in winter. Pets must be on a leash and are allowed only in the campground, not on trails. The property is pretty and shady. This site is closest to the Happy Isle Nature Center. No seclusion or peace and quiet in the summer.

**Wawona Campground.** Wawona, Yosemite National Park. ☎ **800/436-7275.** 100 tent and RV sites. Reservations required May–Sept. $15. Piped water. Flush toilets, fireplaces, and picnic tables. A grocery store, propane gas, disposal station, and horseback riding facility are nearby. Pets permitted. The campground can also accommodate pack animals; call for information. From Wawona, drive 1 mile north of Hwy. 41 to the campground.

Not much seclusion but a pretty place to stay beneath towering trees. The campground is near the Mariposa Grove of Giant Sequoias and Wawona. It's also close to the Merced River, which offers some of the better fishing in the park.

**White Wolf Campground.** White Wolf, Yosemite National Park. ☎ **209/372-0200** for recorded information. 87 tent and RV sites. No reservations. $10. Piped water. Flush toilets, picnic tables, and fireplaces. Showers available at nearby White Wolf Lodge for $2. A small grocery is nearby. Pets permitted. Evening ranger programs. Open July–Sept. From Buck Meadows, drive 20 miles east on Hwy. 120, bear left, and drive 15 miles to White Wolf Rd. and turn left. The road dead-ends at the campground.

Secluded in a forest, this is a nice place to stay for several days with easy access to nearby hiking. The trails here lead to several lakes, including Grant Lake and Lukens Lake. There's a dirt road to Harden Lake, and beyond that, a trail to Smith Peak, which overlooks the Hetch Hetchy Reservoir. Mosquitoes are fierce in the summer. The bathrooms can get neglected.

**Yosemite Creek Campground.** Yosemite National Park. ☎ **209/372-0200** for recorded information. 75 tent sites. No reservations. $6. No piped water. Pit toilets, fireplaces, and picnic tables. Pets permitted. Open July–Sept. From Buck Meadows, drive 30 miles east on Hwy. 120 to the campground road. It's 5 miles down the road to the campground.

This quaint place set along Yosemite Creek is a good place to check if the park is full and you need a place to stay. It's a lesser-known campground where you do everything yourself and for that reason it frequently has space available.

# OUTSIDE THE PARK

Yosemite is surrounded by national forests that offer comparable campgrounds to the ones in the park, albeit less crowded. There are also private campgrounds, which will cost you.

## ALONG HIGHWAY 120 EASTBOUND

**Lumsden.** Stanislaus National Forest. ☎ **209/962-7825** for information. 11 tent sites. No reservations. No fee. No piped water. Vault toilets, picnic tables, and fireplaces. Open Apr–Oct. From Groveland, take Hwy. 120 about 7.5 miles (about $^1/_2$-mile east of the turn for county road J20). Turn left and drive 1 mile. Turn right onto a dirt road and drive 6 miles to the campground.

The campground is along the Tuolumne River, on a scenic stretch between the Hetch Hetchy and Don Pedro reservoirs. It's at an elevation of about 1,500 feet and summers are unbelievably hot.

**Lumsden Bridge.** Stanislaus National Forest. ☎ **209/962-7825** for information. 9 tent sites. No reservations. No fee. No piped water. Vault toilets, picnic tables, and stoves. Open Apr–Oct. From Groveland, take Hwy. 120 east 7.5 miles (about $^1/_2$-mile east of the turn for county road J20). Turn left and drive 1 mile. Turn right onto a dirt road and drive 7.5 miles to the campground.

A fave of rafters because the location is close to some of the Tuolumne River's best stretches. The campground is on the riverbank, near some of California's most awesome white water.

**Lost Claim.** Stanislaus National Forest. ☎ **209/962-7925** for information. 10 tent and RV (small) sites. No reservations. $8. Hand-pumped well water. Vault toilets, stoves, and picnic tables. There's a grocery store nearby. Open May–Oct. From Groveland, drive 11 miles east on Hwy. 120.

Easy access but that's about it. The river is nearby and the fish bite, but they're small and hardly seem worth it.

**The Pines.** Stanislaus National Forest. ☎ **209/962-7825** for information. 21 tent and RV sites. No reservations. $9. Piped water May–Oct. Vault toilets, picnic tables, and fireplaces. A grocery store is nearby. From Groveland, take Hwy. 120 east about 8 miles (about a mile east of the turn for county road J20). Turn right onto the campground entrance road and drive a short distance.

The campground is 1.5 miles from the Tuolumne River. It can get scorching hot here during the summer.

**South Fork.** Stanislaus National Forest. ☎ **209/962-7825** for information. 25 tent and RV (small) sites. No reservations. No fee. No piped water. Vault toilets and stoves. A grocery store is nearby. Open Apr–Nov. From Buck Meadows, drive 13 miles east on Hwy. 120 to Evergreen Rd. Turn left and drive 5 miles to the campground.

This is a pretty spot along the Tuolumne's middle fork. It's an easy ride, yet far enough out of the way.

## ALONG HIGHWAY 140 WESTBOUND

**Indian Flat.** Sierra National Forest. ☎ **209/683-4665** for information. 35 tent and RV sites. No reservations. $9. Piped water. Vault toilets, fireplaces, and picnic tables. A grocery store is nearby. From El Portal, drive 4 miles south on Hwy. 140. From Mariposa, it's 24 miles north.

A pretty place next to the Merced. There are great swimming holes and access is easy.

**Jerseydale.** Sierra National Forest. ☎ **209/683-4665** for information. 12 tent sites; 2 can accommodate RVs. No reservations. No fee. Piped water. Vault toilets, fireplaces, and picnic tables. A grocery store is nearby. Open May–Nov. From Mariposa, drive about 5 miles north on Hwy. 140 to Acorn Lodge. Turn right on Triangle Rd. and drive 6 miles to Darrah. Turn left and drive 3 miles to the campground adjacent to the Jerseydale Ranger Station.

Great location to explore and be out of the way of crowds. A dirt road heads east into the Chowchilla Mountains. There is also access to the Merced River via a trailhead 6 miles north of the ranger station.

**Yosemite–Mariposa KOA Campground.** 6323 Hwy. 140, Mariposa. ☎ **209/966-2201.** 40 tent sites, 30 motor home sites with full hookups, 10 sites for tents or motor homes. $18–$30. Piped water. Flush toilets, showers, sanitary disposal station, laundry, store, propane gas, swimming pool, and playground. From Mariposa, drive 7 miles northeast on Hwy. 140 to 6323 Hwy. 140.

A good save if Yosemite is full. The campground is 28 miles from the park entrance and near the Merced River.

## ALONG HIGHWAY 41

**Summerdale.** Sierra National Forest. ☎ **209/683-4665** for information. 30 tent and RV sites. No reservations. $9. Piped water. Vault toilets, fireplaces, and picnic tables. A grocery store is nearby. Open May–Oct. From Fish Camp, drive a mile north on Hwy. 41 to the campground.

A pretty spot, but usually full by noon on Friday. It's on the south fork of the Merced River and its location makes it a prime spot for overflow Yosemite visitors. Elevation is 5,000 feet.

**Summit Camp.** Sierra National Forest. ☎ **209/683-4665** for information. 2 tent sites. No reservations. No fee. Piped water. Vault toilets, fireplaces, and picnic tables. Open June–Nov. From Oakhurst, drive northwest to Fish Camp. Go west on Forest Rd. for about 5 miles to the campground.

This tiny little campground that's often overlooked is a great place to crash if Yosemite is full. At 5,800 feet, this site is well into the Chowchilla Mountains. It's also 3 miles from Big Creek.

## ALONG HIGHWAY 120 WESTBOUND

**Aspen Grove.** Hwy. 120, along Lee Vining Creek. ☎ **760/872-4240** for information. 58 tent and RV (small) sites. No reservations. $5. No piped water.

Pit toilets. Pets permitted. Open May–Oct. From Lee Vining, drive 6 miles west on Hwy. 120.

This is a high country campground set along Lee Vining Creek at an amazing 8,000 feet. It's primitive and near Mono Lake.

**Big Bend.** Inyo National Forest. ☎ **760/872-4240** for information. 18 tent and RV sites. No reservations. $7. Piped water. Flush toilets. A grocery is nearby. Open May to mid-Oct. From Lee Vining, drive 7 miles west on Hwy. 120.

Located on the eastern Sierra, this campground is sparse but breathtaking. It's located along Lee Vining Creek at an elevation of 7,800 feet.

**Ellery Lake.** Inyo National Forest. ☎ **760/872-4240** for information. 13 tent and RV sites. No reservations. $7. Piped water. Flush toilets, fireplaces, and picnic tables. A grocery store is nearby. Open June to mid-Oct. From Lee Vining, drive 9 miles west on Hwy. 120.

Another series of small, pretty camps, this time along Ellery Lake, which is a short distance from Tioga Lake.

**Junction.** Inyo National Forest. ☎ **760/872-4240** for information. 10 tent and RV sites. No reservations. No fee. No piped water. Vault toilets, fireplaces, and picnic tables. Open June–Oct. From Lee Vining, drive 10 miles west on Hwy. 120.

A little-known campground right off Highway 120. It's near Ellery and Tioga lakes, and the Tioga Tarns Nature Trail is nearby.

**Lee Vining Creek Campgrounds.** Lee Vining. ☎ **760/872-4240** for information. 129 tent and RV sites. No reservations. $5. No piped water. Pit toilets. Pets permitted. Open May–Oct. From Lee Vining, drive 4–5 miles west along Hwy. 120 to this series of 4 campgrounds.

This is a group of four campgrounds clustered along Highway 120. It's basically just a place to rest your head for a fee. The campgrounds are set along Lee Vining Creek.

**Saddlebag Lake.** Inyo National Forest. ☎ **760/872-4240** for information. 22 tent and RV sites. No reservations. $7. Piped water. Flush toilets, fireplaces, and picnic tables. A grocery store is nearby. Open June to mid-Oct. From Lee Vining, drive 10 miles west on Hwy. 120. Turn north on Saddlebag Lake Rd. and drive about 2 miles to the campground.

This is the highest drive-to camp in the state at 10,000 feet. It's situated along Saddlebag Lake and near Lee Vining Creek. It is beautiful and a good place to stay a while, or head out into the wilderness with a backpack.

**Tioga Lake.** Inyo National Forest. ☎ **760/872-4240** for information. 13 tent sites. No reservations. $7. Piped water. Flush toilets, fireplaces, and picnic tables. Open June–Oct. From Lee Vining, drive 10 miles west on Hwy. 120.

This is a good spot to camp if Tuolumne Meadows is full. It's at 9,700 feet and is a pretty camp on the eastern Sierra.

## 3   Where to Eat

We're not sure much proper "dining" goes on around these parts, but there are a dozen places to please your palate in the valley and a handful in the rest of the park. Some are good, a few are wonderful, and all are overpriced. Ah, but what price can be put on feasting in the wilderness, in the shadow of granite giants, in one of the most popular places on the planet? Finding great food outside Yosemite isn't impossible, but it'll take some work. More common are the average restaurants and cafes, where you can grab something in a pinch and again pay more than it's worth. These places are everywhere, particularly along Highways 140 and 41. However, there are some good buys, quirky places, and excellent establishments along each route.

### IN THE VALLEY

**Ahwahnee Dining Room.** Ahwahnee Hotel, Yosemite Valley. ☎ **209/ 372-1489.** Dinner reservations required. Breakfast $6–$15, lunch $9–$13, dinner $10–$25. CB, DC, DISC, JCB, MC, V. Daily 7–10:30am, 11:30am–3pm, and 5:30–9pm. Shuttle bus stop No. 4. GOURMET CUISINE.

Dining here takes your breath away. Even if you are a died-in-the-wool, down-to-the-earth, sleep-under-the-stars backpacker, the Ahwahnee Dining Room will not fail to make an impression. This is where the great outdoors meets four-star cuisine. With understated elegance, the cavernous dining room, its candelabra chandeliers hanging from the 34-foot-tall beamed ceiling, seems intimate once you're seated at a table. Don't be fooled—it seats 450. The walk from the entrance to the table is one long stroll that sets the restaurant's atmosphere. Now open the menu. How about Salmon Ahwahnee, which comes with Dungeness crab with béarnaise sauce and wild rice for $19.95. Or rack of lamb with rosemary polenta for $24.95. Or grilled stuffed quail for $8.85. Or New York steak buried under a trio of mushrooms and served with herb-roasted potatoes for $23. That represents a sliver of the selections offered on various dinner menus, which shift frequently. Don't forget dessert. The crème de bole is to die for. Breakfast includes a mouthwatering selection of omelets, frittatas (both $9.50), and house specialties, such as a thick apple crepe filled with raspberry puree for $7.25. Lunch sandwiches range from a portobello mushroom sandwich for $10 to pasta salad with tomato and fresh mozzarella for $11.50. The

Ahwahnee also has a tremendous wine list. If you're feeling generous, try the Silver Oak cabernet. An evening dress code requires men to wear a coat and tie. The tie is often forgiven.

**Curry Cafeteria.** Curry Village. $4–$12. CB, DC, DISC, JCB, MC, V. Daily 7–10am and 5:30–8pm. Shuttle bus stop Nos. 1, 14, and 15. CAFETERIA.

Starving? Eat here. Otherwise, go to great lengths to stay away. It's not that the food is bad, but the prices are extreme. While there's something here for everyone—big breakfast, small nibble, you name it—the shell shock of paying $20 for breakfast for two (and meager breakfasts they were) requires advanced preparation. This place is short on atmosphere and long on dollar signs. Yosemite Concession Services, with all its know-how, should be ashamed.

**Curry Hamburger Stand.** Curry Village. $3–$4.50. No credit cards. Daily 11am–4pm. Closed in winter. Shuttle bus stop Nos. 1, 14, and 15. BURGERS.

Your basic burger joint. This burger stand also offers chicken sandwiches and outdoor seating. It's a quick place for a quick bite. Try an order of fries—they're huge.

**Curry Village Pizza Patio.** Curry Village, Yosemite Valley. Pizza $8–$14. CB, DC, DISC, JCB, MC, V. Mon–Fri 5–9pm, Sat–Sun noon–9pm. Shuttle bus stop Nos. 1, 14, and 15. PIZZA.

Need to watch ESPN? This is the place, but you may have to wait in line. The alternative to the big-screen room is the scenic outdoors with its large umbrellas, table service, and Mother Nature, plus or minus a hundred kids. But one of the park's few big screens awaits inside, and if you're a sports buff this is the place to be. The lounge also taps a few brews—nothing special but a mix aimed to please. This is a great place to chill after a long day.

**Degnan's Deli.** Yosemite Village. $4–$5. CB, DC, DISC, JCB, MC, V. Daily 8am–6pm. Shuttle bus stop Nos. 3, 5, and 10. DELI.

A solid delicatessen with a large selection of sandwiches made to order as well as incidentals. It's half market, half deli. The sandwiches are generous. Sometimes the line to order gets long, but it moves quickly. There's also a selection of premade stuff—salads, sandwiches, desserts—in addition to snacks to stuff in a knapsack before heading out for the day. Degnan's also has a decent beer and wine selection.

**Degnan's Pasta.** Yosemite Village. Entrees $4–$7. CB, DC, DISC, JCB, MC, V. Mon–Fri 11am–2pm and 5–8pm, Sat–Sun 11:30am–8pm. Shuttle bus stop Nos. 3, 5, and 10. PIZZA/PASTA.

Adjacent to Degnan's Deli and Degnan's Pizzeria and Ice Cream (a gastronomic monopoly in Yosemite?), this is one of the valley's newest editions. Formerly the Loft Restaurant, Degnan's Pasta is a good family place. The atmosphere is cheery. There's a central fireplace and high-beamed ceilings. The pasta menu features a variety of pasta sauces that frequently rotate. Hot bread sticks, salads, and desserts are made fresh daily.

**Degnan's Pizzeria and Ice Cream.** Yosemite Village. Pizza $7–$13. CB, DC, DISC, JCB, MC, V. Daily 11:30am–5:30pm. Shuttle bus stop Nos. 3, 5, and 10. PIZZA.

Adjacent to Degnan's Deli, this place offers pizza and ice cream. The pizza is definitely not baked in a brick wood-fired oven, but it's pizza. The ice-cream scoops are small, but it's ice cream.

**Garden Terrace.** Yosemite Lodge. $7.75 flat price, $5.50 for ages 5–15, $1.50 for ages 1–5. CB, DC, JCB, MC, V. Daily 11am–9pm. Shuttle bus stop No. 8. SALAD BAR.

This all-you-can-eat soup, salad, and pasta bar may be the best deal in the valley. It includes 30 selections of homemade soups, fresh salads, and baked goods. Pasta selections vary and can range from spaghetti to manicotti. Carved meats are also available for an additional $3.75. A double-pane skylight and windows allow plenty of sunlight. The restaurant just opened in mid-1997 and has received good reviews from visitors as convenient and a good deal.

**Mountain Room Restaurant.** Yosemite Lodge. Entrees $12–$20. CB, DC, DISC, JCB, MC, V. Daily 6–9pm. Shuttle bus stop No. 8. AMERICAN

The best thing about this restaurant is the view. The food's good, too, but the floor-to-ceiling windows overlooking Yosemite Falls are spectacular. There's not a bad seat in the house. The restaurant opened in 1997 and is a worthy alternative to the prices charged at The Ahwahnee. We spent $55 on dinner for two, including wine. The grilled chicken breast was flavorful and moist, as was the Idaho trout—but watch out for a few bones. Meals come with vegetables and bread. Soup or salad is extra. There is a children's menu, entrees for vegetarians, and an amazing dessert tray. The Mountain Room also has a good wine list.

**Village Grill.** Yosemite Village. Burgers and sandwiches $3–$4.50. No credit cards. Summer only, daily 7:30am–4pm. Shuttle bus stop Nos. 3, 5, and 10. BURGERS.

Your basic burger joint. The Village Grill also offers chicken sandwiches and outdoor seating. It's a quick place for a quick bite.

**Yosemite Lodge Cafeteria.** Yosemite Lodge. Entrees $4–$12. CB, DC, DISC, JCB, MC, V. Daily 6:30–10am, 11:30am–2pm, and 5–8:30pm. Shuttle bus stop No. 8. CAFETERIA.

Breakfast, lunch, and dinner, but it comes at a price. The food is thoroughly mediocre, but it's convenient. It's also grossly overpriced, but that doesn't seem to bother the hundreds of people who eat here every day. There's enough room here to accommodate a family. Kids love the place. And if you're packing the little nippers, this may be a good buy after all.

## ELSEWHERE IN THE PARK

**Tuolumne Meadows Lodge.** Tuolumne Meadows, Hwy. 120. ☎ **209/ 372-8413.** Reservations required for dinner. Breakfast $2–$6, dinner $4–$16. CB, DC, DISC, JCB, MC, V. Daily 7–9am and 6–8pm. AMERICAN.

One of the two restaurants in Yosemite's high country, the lodge offers something for everyone. The breakfast menu offers eggs, pancakes, fruit, and granola. The Meadow Scramble is a mouthful of eggs, ham, and veggies served with potatoes and toast. Lighter fare is also available. Granola, yogurt, and oatmeal are staples. Dinners always include a beef, chicken, fish, pasta, and vegetarian specialty, all of which change frequently. The quality can swing. The prime rib and New York steak are consistently edible. There's also a children's menu.

**Wawona Hotel Dining Room.** Wawona, Hwy. 41, Wawona. ☎ **209/ 375-1425.** Breakfast and lunch $4–$7, dinner $12–$20. CB, DC, DISC, JCB, MC, V. Mon–Sat 7:30–10am, noon–1:30pm, and 5:30–8:30pm; Sun 7:30am– 1:30pm (brunch) and 5:30–8:30pm. AMERICAN.

The Wawona dining room mirrors the hotel's ambience—wide open, lots of windows and sunlight. And the fare is great. For breakfast choose from a variety of items, including the Par Three, a combo of French toast or pancakes, eggs, and bacon or sausage— just what you need before hitting the golf course. Lunch is a buffet that changes seasonally. Dinner is delectable. In addition to some amazing entrees, such as roast duckling with cranberry orange glaze, grilled polenta, and Indian Tom's South Fork Trout, there are amazing appetizers. The stuffed mushroom caps, grilled artichoke, and gulf shrimp cocktail are sumptuous.

**White Wolf Lodge.** White Wolf, Hwy. 120. ☎ **209/372-8416.** Reservations required for dinner. Breakfast $4–$7, dinner $10–$17. CB, DC, DISC, JCB, MC, V. Daily 7–9am and 6–8:30pm. AMERICAN.

Breakfast offers a choice of eggs, pancakes, omelets, or biscuits and gravy. Dinner always includes a beef, chicken, fish, pasta, and vegetarian dish. The actual menu items vary. The portions are large, the staff is wonderful and enthusiastic, but alas, the food is mediocre.

## OUTSIDE THE PARK

**Branding Iron.** 640 W. 16th St., Merced. ☎ **209/722-1822.** Reservations suggested. Entrees $13–$20. AE, MC, V. Mon–Fri 11:30am–2pm and 5:30–9pm, Sat–Sun 5:30–9pm. STEAK/SEAFOOD.

Merced's most popular steak house, the Branding Iron is in the heart of town, beyond big green awnings. The prime rib is a house favorite, but the rest of the menu gets rave reviews as well. Entrees come with soup, salad, vegetables, and potatoes.

**Castillo's Mexican Food.** 4995 5th St., Mariposa. ☎ **209/742-4413.** Reservations recommended in summer. Entrees $8–$15. MC, V. Daily 11am–9pm. From eastbound Hwy. 140, turn right on 5th St. Drive 1 block. The restaurant is on your right. MEXICAN.

Established in 1955, this cheerful, cozy cantina serves breakfast, lunch, and dinner all day. The food is good and portions are plentiful. Entrees come with salad, rice, and beans, and can also be ordered à la carte. The house specialty, the Tostada Compuesta, fills a hungry belly. A children's menu is available. The service is great. Chips, salsa, and guacamole arrived before we'd removed our coats.

**Charles Street Dinner House.** 5043 Hwy. 140, Mariposa. ☎ **209/966-2366.** Reservations recommended in summer. Entrees $15–$50. AE, DISC, MC, V. Tues–Sat 5–9pm. Closed Jan. STEAK/SEAFOOD.

The owner here likes to describe this place as "gourmet." Let's just say it's a hearty place with hearty food and leave it at that. Whatever it is, the Charles Street Dinner House is straight out of the Old West. The huge wagon wheel in the front window makes that clear. Inside is a kitschy compilation of family photos and plastic flowers. The menu covers everything that American food is supposed to be, in an attempt to appeal to international travelers. There is a wide selection of steak and seafood dishes, plus nightly specials, and all entrees come with soup, salad, and bread. The food can be mediocre. The New York steak was unimpressive and the Scallone—the chef's concoction of abalone and scallops—lacked flavor. At an average of $20 a meal, it seems customers deserve a little more. It didn't help that the selection of wines and beers was weak. The service was quite good, however.

**Groveland Hotel's Victorian Room.** 18767 Hwy. 120, Groveland. ☎ **800/273-3314** or 209/962-4000. Fax 209/962-6674. Reservations suggested.

Entrees $13–$20. AE, CB, DC, DISC, JCB, MC, V. Daily 6–11pm in summer and 6–8:30pm in winter. CALIFORNIAN.

With the unique combination of four-star food and a one-star dress code, this restaurant offers casual dining at its finest. The menu has something for everyone and is constantly changing to reflect what's fresh and in season. There's a sumptuous rack of lamb marinated in rosemary and garlic, salmon with fresh cucumber and dill, chicken breast with fresh fruit salsa, and more. The menu usually has a fresh seafood and pasta special as well as an innkeeper's special. All entrees are served with soup or salad and fresh warm bread. There's an adjacent bar and what has to be one of the most extensive wine lists in the Sierra. Now, that's not saying much, but this one is solid and reflects innkeepers Peggy and Grover Mosely's attention to detail. The restaurant is also handicap accessible. The Groveland Hotel is an excellent place to stay the night.

**Hotel Charlotte.** 18736 Hwy. 120, Groveland. ☎ **800/961-7799** or 209/962-7872. Reservations suggested in the summer. Entrees $11–$16. AE, MC, V. Daily 6–10pm in summer and 5–9pm in winter. AMERICAN.

Casual dinners are offered in the small dining room of this quaint hotel. The menu includes mostly meat and fish dishes. Daily specials range from halibut with lemon to barbecued baby-back ribs. Vegetarians can choose from pasta primavera or stir-fry. All meals include soup, salad, veggies, potato or rice, and bread. There is also a full bar and a healthy wine list.

**Iron Door Saloon and Grill.** Hwy. 120, Groveland. ☎ **209/962-6244.** Entrees $4–$14. DISC, MC, V. Daily 11am–9pm. BURGERS.

You'll miss this place if you blink. Groveland is about 3 blocks long and this is the best watering hole in town. It's a funky, fun, comfortable place to hang out for a few hours if (a) you're sick of traffic, (b) you're sick of lines, or (c) you just want to stall before hooking up with your entire family for a weekend getaway in one of the most crowded places around. The saloon and grill are in adjacent rooms. The bar is stocked with history, from the hunting trophies on the walls to the dollar bills pinned to the ceiling (go ahead, ask). The food is strictly burgers, fries, and shakes and it's all good. There are 27 burger variations, including buffalo meat and veggie tofu. There are kids' offerings and salads. The milk shakes are dreamy. There's live music most Fridays and Saturdays. This is almost always a good place, the exception being Thursday night—the family karaoke night that for some unknown reason compels hoards of teens to take to the stage to sing tunes from the 1970s and 1980s (think *Saturday Night Fever*).

**Lenny's.** 1052 W. Main St., Merced. ☎ **209/722-0350.** Entrees $10–$16. AE, MC, V. Mon–Fri 7am–9:30pm, Sat 7am–10pm, Sun 9am–9pm. ITALIAN.

A popular Merced restaurant that serves old-world favorites. Recipes on the menu here have been passed down for generations, but the owner has added a few American twists of his own. The lunch buffet, loaded with pastas and at least 15 other dishes, seems the best bargain in town. Dinners are more elaborate, with all sauces and sausages made on the premises. Lenny's also serves 150 kinds of beer and has an espresso bar.

**Meadows Ranch Cafe.** 5024 Hwy. 140, Mariposa. ☎ **209/966-4242.** Reservations recommended on summer weekends. Breakfast $3–$6, lunch $4–$6, dinner $6–$16, pizza $7.95. MC, V. Mon–Sat 7am–10pm in summer, 7am–9pm in winter, Sun 9am–noon. AMERICAN.

A great place for a quick bite or a full meal. The food is wholesome and fresh. The coffee is great. Breakfasts include a variety of egg dishes, omelets, and breakfast burritos—a toss of eggs, meat, veggies, and cheese rolled in a warm tortilla. Lunch includes a selection of more than two dozen sandwiches on a variety of breads. Dinner includes pizzas, pasta, and a few grilled selections, including grilled lemon herb chicken breast and barbecued beef. The owners recently began a much-anticipated Sunday brunch that was expecting rave reviews. The 100-year-old dining room is adjacent to the cafe's new brew pub, where patrons can watch the brewing process.

**PJ's Cafe and Pizzeria.** 18986 Hwy. 120, Groveland. ☎ **209/962-7501.** Entrees $3–$7, pizza $5–$15. No credit cards. Daily 7am–8pm.

Best known as a pizzeria and burger house, PJ's serves a hearty breakfast with an eye toward helping all of us lower our fat and cholesterol intake. That being said, you can still order bacon and eggs without getting the evil eye. Breakfast comes with potatoes and toast. All meat and egg dishes use a special low-cholesterol oil. PJ's also uses only lean ground chuck in its chili, taco meat, and meat sauces, which are available for lunch and dinner. The pizzas are interesting, ranging from a create-your-own to the yummy pesto-chicken-artichoke-tomato combination.

## PICNIC & CAMPING SUPPLIES

If you forget something, chances are you'll be able to get it in the valley. But elsewhere in the park it's tough to find equipment. The best place to get supplies and camping equipment in the valley is the **Yosemite Village Store.** The **Yosemite Lodge Gift Shop** and **Curry Village General Store** stock some supplies. The **Mountaineering Shop** at Curry Village sells clothing and equipment for day hikes as well as backcountry excursions.

# 6

# Exploring Sequoia/Kings Canyon

*M*ost of these parks is wilderness, accessible only by foot. There are no roads crisscrossing the parks and no entrance from the east. The three main entrances all enter the park from the southwest and leave much of Sequoia/Kings Canyon undeveloped. The park service likes it that way. Here, unlike Yosemite, are guardians determined to protect their charge from the hazards of overpopularity. If you visit here after staying in Yosemite, be prepared for a shock. There are some, but not four dozen, ranger-led hikes. There is no shuttle bus with bus drivers pointing out landmarks like a tour guide. There are no special events, nothing aimed at bringing more folks in than would otherwise come just to see the beauty and majesty of the largest living things on earth. In fact, the Park Service says there aren't even regular commercial tours led through the parks. None of this is likely to change any time soon. The Park Service here is determined to learn from Yosemite's mistakes and so are residents in nearby towns. This is nature, not Disneyland. Expect far fewer people, far less to entertain, and lots more to explore at your leisure.

## 1 Essentials

### ACCESS/ENTRY POINTS

You'll find the Big Stump Entrance (Kings Canyon National Park) via Highway 180 and the Ash Mountain Entrance (Sequoia National Park) via Highway 198, both from the west. Continuing east on Highway 180 also brings you to an entrance near Cedar Grove Village in the canyon itself, which is open only in summer. See the map on page 23 for general highway access information. To access the Mineral King area of Sequoia National Park, take the steep, twisting Mineral King Road off Highway 198, just a few miles outside the Ash Mountain Entrance.

## VISITOR CENTERS & INFORMATION

There are three visitor centers in the parks where you can buy books and maps. The biggest is in Sequoia National Park at Lodgepole (☎ 209/565-3782) and it's open spring, summer, and fall. It's 4.5 miles north of Giant Forest Village, where a new museum of the sequoias is under development and scheduled to open early in the next century. Lodgepole includes exhibits on geology, wildlife, air quality, and park history. The Foothills Visitor Center (☎ 209/565-3134) just inside the Ash Mountain Entrance on Highway 198 is open all year and includes exhibits on the chaparral region's ecosystem. The visitor center in Grant Grove, Kings Canyon National Park (☎ 209/335-2856), includes exhibits on logging and the role of fire in the forests. It's also open year-round.

## FEES

It costs $10 per car per week to enter the park or $5 for individuals walking in or arriving by bicycle.

It costs $6 to $14 a night to camp in the park. Most campgrounds are first-come, first-served. Only Lodgepole has a reservation system, and then only from Memorial Day to mid-October. Grant, Dorst, and Cedar Grove group campsites must be reserved by mail. Mail requests to either Sunset Group Sites at Grant Grove, Canyon View Group Sites at Cedar Grove, at P.O. Box 926, Kings Canyon National Park, CA 93633, or to Dorst Group Sites, P.O. Box C, Lodgepole, Sequoia N.P., CA 93262.

## REGULATIONS

In Sequoia/Kings Canyon, there is a 14-day camping limit from June 14 to September 14, with a ceiling of 30 camping days per year. In general, a maximum of six people and two vehicles may stay at each campground. Check campsite bulletin boards for additional regulations. Some campgrounds close in winter (see chart on page 132). Pets are allowed in a few campgrounds, but they must be on a leash and are not allowed on any trails. Proper food storage is required due to the presence of black bears.

## SPECIAL DISCOUNTS & PASSES

The Sequoia/Kings Canyon yearly pass sells for $20. The National Park Service also sells the Golden Eagle Pass, which costs $50 for a year and provides entrance to all national parks. Senior citizens (62 and older) can purchase a lifetime Golden Age Pass for $10 that admits them every time from the date of purchase. The blind and

132permanently disabled are eligible for the free Golden Access Pass. Passes are available at the gates, or a ranger will provide directions to park purchase stations.

## FAST FACTS: Sequoia & Kings Canyon National Parks

**ATMs**   At the moment, there are two bank machines in Sequoia/ Kings Canyon. In Sequoia there's one inside the Giant Forest Market (scheduled to close in October of 1998), and in Kings Canyon you'll find one in Grant Grove, in the lobby between the gift shop and restaurant.

**Car Trouble/Towing Services**   Call ☎ **911** for all emergencies, including car trouble. The operator will alert a ranger for assistance.

**Climate**   See chapter 2.

**Emergencies**   Call ☎ **911.**

**Gas Stations**   There are no gas stations within Sequoia and Kings Canyon national parks at this time, however, a gas station can be found at the Kings Canyon Lodge in Sequoia National Forest, between Grant Grove and Cedar Grove. There are also gas stations in the town of Three Rivers on Highway 198.

**Laundromats**   You'll find a laundry at the Lodgepole Market Center in Sequoia National Park and at Cedar Grove Village in Kings Canyon.

**Maps**   General maps are handed out at park entrances. Use these to plan your drive around the parks. Many of the shorter trails are well marked, but when planning hikes or exploring the backcountry, pick up a topographical map at a visitor center or ranger station. For $1.50 you can buy an excellent pocket map that highlights main features and trails. The maps, published by the Sequoia Natural History Association, cover Cedar Grove, Giant Forest, Grant Grove, Mineral King, and Lodgepole– Wolverton.

**Medical/Dental Clinics**   All emergencies and injuries are referred to doctors and dentists in nearby Visalia or Three Rivers.

**Permits**   Required for all overnight camping in the backcountry (see chapter 7). In Sequoia/Kings Canyon, call ☎ **209/565-3341.** Information is also available online at **www.nps.gov/seki/**.

**Post Offices**   There is a post office at Lodgepole Market Center in Sequoia National Park and at Grant Grove in Kings Canyon.

**Supplies**   In Sequoia, the widest selection can be found at the Lodgepole Market Center. Smaller markets with food and supplies are located at Giant Forest, Grant Grove, and Cedar Grove.

**Weather**   For Sequoia/Kings Canyon, call ☎ **209/565-3341,** then press 4.

## 2   Orientation

The parks are roughly equidistant (5 hours by car) from both San Francisco and Los Angeles. Kings Canyon National Park is north of Sequoia National Park. Kings Canyon has the developed areas of Grant Grove and Cedar Grove. It is also nearest to Yosemite and Fresno. In Sequoia, you'll find the Giant Forest sequoia grove, as well as Lodgepole, the Foothills, and Mineral King. The main entrance (for all except Mineral King) is on Highway 198, via Ash Mountain through Visalia and Three Rivers. While it's impossible to cross through the parks from west to east, a north–south road known as the Generals Highway connects Grant Grove in Kings Canyon National Park with Giant Forest in Sequoia National Park. The Generals Highway runs between two Giant Sequoias named after generals—the General Grant Tree and the General Sherman Tree. It's an hour-long drive between the two. Another choice is the road to Mineral King, which breaks off Highway 198, cuts through Sequoia National Forest, and heads 11 miles to the Lookout Point Entrance. From here it's another 15 miles to Mineral King. This steep, narrow, twisting dead-end road is closed in winter and does not reconnect with any other park roadways.

### INTRODUCTION TO SEQUOIA NATIONAL PARK

The best-known stand of sequoias in the world can be found in **Giant Forest,** part of Sequoia National Park. Named in 1875 by explorer and environmentalist John Muir, this area consists mostly of huge meadows and a large grove of giant trees. At the northern edge of the grove, you can't miss the General Sherman Tree, considered the largest living thing on the planet, although it is neither the tallest nor widest. Its size is noteworthy because of the tree's volume—experts estimate the weight of its trunk at about 1,387 tons. It is believed to be between 2,300 and 2,700 years old, *and it's still growing.* The General Sherman Tree is 274.9 feet tall, measures 102.6 feet around at its base, and its largest branch measures 6.8 feet in diameter. Every year, it adds enough new wood to make another 60-foot-tall tree. The tree is part of the 2-mile Congress Trail, a foot trail that includes groups of trees with names such as the Senate and the House.

Another interesting stop in Giant Forest is **Tharp's Log,** a cabin named after the first non–Native American settler in the area, Hale Tharp, who grazed cattle among the Giant Sequoias and built a summer cabin in the 1860s from a fallen sequoia hollowed by fire. It is the oldest cabin remaining in the park.

You'll also encounter two kitschy items in the Giant Forest vicinity—**Tunnel Log** is a toppled tree that you can drive *through,* and **Auto Log** is a tree that you can drive *on.*

Nearby **Crescent Meadow** is a pristine clearing dotted with wildflowers and tall grasses. A trail (described later in this chapter) wraps around the meadow. This is also the trailhead for several backcountry hikes.

Also in the area is **Moro Rock,** the large granite dome we mentioned earlier that's worth ascending. It takes about a half-hour to get up and down. From the top, Moro Rock offers one of the most spectacular views of the dark and barren Great Western Divide, which includes the Kaweah Range. The divide is one of two crests in the southern Sierra Nevada, but not officially the main crest, which lies to the east and obscured from view.

South of the Giant Forest is the turnoff for **Crystal Cave,** one of more than 100 caves in the parks and one of just two in the area that offer guided tours (Boyden Cavern is in the neighboring national forest). The cave is composed of limestone that has turned to marble and is full of stalactites and stalagmites. To reach the entrance, drive 7 miles down the narrow winding road (RVs, trailers, and buses are prohibited), and the cave entrance is an additional 15-minute walk down a steep path. The Sequoia Natural History Association conducts 45-minute tours daily between 11am and 4pm from June through Labor Day, and less often in May and late September. Tickets are not sold at the cave but rather at the Lodgepole and Foothills visitor centers. The cost is $5 for adults, $2.50 for children and seniors with a Golden Eagle pass, and free for children under 6. Information is also available by telephone (☎ **209/565-3759**). It gets cold underground, so bring a sweater or jacket.

In summer, Giant Forest has a market, restaurant, and lodging—but only through 1998. Remember that all amenities here are being phased out, with the last of them expected to close in October 1998. They will eventually be replaced at the Wuksachi Village.

**Lodgepole,** the most developed area in both parks, lies just northeast of Giant Forest on the Generals Highway. Here, you'll find the

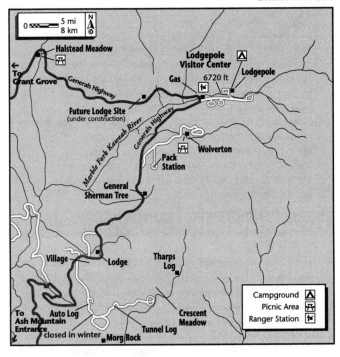

largest visitor center in both parks. There is a large market, several places to eat, the Walter Fry Nature Center, a laundry, a post office, and showers.

South of Giant Forest about 16 miles is the region of the park known as the **Foothills.** Located near the Ash Mountain Entrance, the Foothills has a visitor center, several campgrounds, and Hospital Rock, a large boulder with ancient pictographs that are believed to have been painted by the Monache Indians who once lived here. Nearby are about 50 grinding spots once used to smash acorns into flour. A short trail leads down to a beautiful spot along the Kaweah River where the water gushes over rapids into deep, clear pools. Hospital Rock also has a nice picnic area.

**Mineral King** is a pristine, undeveloped region in the southern part of the park. This high-mountain valley was carved by glaciers and is bordered by the tall peaks of the Great Western Divide. To reach this area, patient drivers must follow the marked highway sign 3 miles outside Sequoia National Park's Ash Mountain Entrance. From the turnoff to Mineral King, it's a 28-mile trip that makes 698 tight turns and takes 1¹/₂ hours to drive. Trailers, RVs, and buses are not allowed. The road is closed in winter. Mineral King was annexed to the park in 1978, but a silver prospector named it in the 1800s. The rocky landscape is as colorful as a rainbow—red and orange shales mix with white marble and black metamorphic shale and granite. In winter, this area is prone to avalanches. The most prominent point in the area is Sawtooth Peak, which reaches 12,343 feet. Sawtooth and other peaks in this region resemble the Rocky Mountains more than the rest of the Sierra Nevada because they are made of metamorphic rocks. The trails in Mineral King begin at 7,500 feet and climb. Park rangers sometimes conduct hikes around here. The best way to experience Mineral King is to stay overnight in one of two nearby campgrounds.

## INTRODUCTION TO KINGS CANYON NATIONAL PARK

With its rugged canyon, huge river, and desolate backcountry, Kings Canyon is considered a hiker's dream. It consists of Grant Grove and Cedar Grove, as well as portions of the Monarch Wilderness and Jennie Lakes Wilderness. One other point of note: Between Grant Grove and Cedar Grove is a stretch of land not in the park but in Sequoia National Forest instead. This region includes Hume Lake, Boyden Cavern, and several campgrounds.

**Grant Grove** is the most crowded region in either park. Not only is it located just a few miles from a main entrance but the area is also a thoroughfare for travelers heading from Giant Forest to the south or Cedar Grove to the east. The grove was designated as General Grant National Park in 1890, and when Kings Canyon National Park was formed in 1940 it was incorporated.

Here you'll find the towering General Grant Tree amid a grove of spectacular Giant Sequoias. The tree was discovered by Joseph Hardin Tomas in 1862 and named 5 years later by Lucretia P. Baker to honor Ulysses S. Grant. The tree measures 267.4 feet tall, 107.6 feet around, and is thought to be the world's third largest living thing, possibly 2,000 years old (just a youngster in this neighborhood!). This tree has been officially declared the "Nation's Christmas Tree" and is the cornerstone of an annual Christmas tree ceremony.

Two and a half miles southwest of the grove is the Big Stump Trail, an instructive hike that can be slightly depressing as it winds among the remains of logged sequoias. Since sequoia wood decays slowly, you'll see century-old leftover piles of sawdust that remain

# Grant Grove

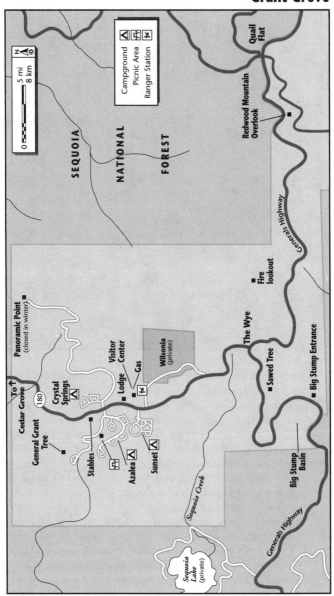

# Cedar Grove

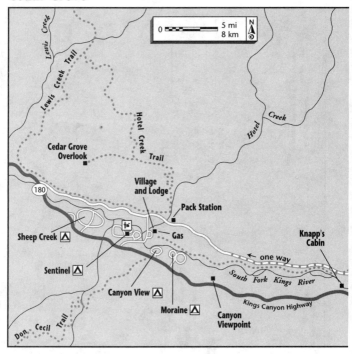

from the logging days. Nearby, Panoramic Point visitors can stand atop a 7,520-foot ledge and see across a large stretch of the Sierra, and across the Kings Canyon. Grant Grove Village also has a restaurant, market, gift shop, and visitor center.

Although in the same park, **Cedar Grove** seems a world away. That this region is around today is sheer luck. There were plans to flood Kings Canyon by damming the Kings River. Today it's an incomprehensible move and one that would have buried Cedar Grove beneath a very deep lake. With that future thwarted, the region stood to become another Yosemite, but people fought hard to prevent that fate and eventually everyone agreed that there are better uses for the Sierra than to convert it to a giant parking garage. Even after the park was established, Cedar Grove was excluded due to the controversy over how this region would be developed. It was finally annexed in 1965 and under a master plan for the area will remain as it is today. One look and you'll see why any other alternative would have been foolish.

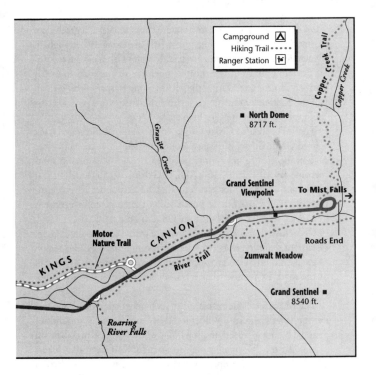

Cedar Grove is covered with lush landscape, tumbling waterfalls, and miles upon miles of solitude. Half the fun is driving through Kings Canyon as its sheer granite walls close around you and the wild South Fork of the Kings River races by. One mile east of the Cedar Grove Village turnoff is Canyon View, where visitors can see the glacially carved U shape of Kings Canyon. Easily accessible nature trails in Cedar Grove include Zumwalt Meadow, Roaring River Falls, and Knapp's Cabin. Zumwalt Meadow is dotted with ponderosa pine and has good views of two rock formations: the Grand Sentinel and North Dome. The top of Grand Sentinel is 8,504 feet above sea level while North Dome, which some say resembles Half Dome in Yosemite, tops out at 8,717 feet. The mile-long trail around the meadow is one of the prettiest in the park. The best place to access this walk is at a parking lot 4.5 miles east of the turnoff for Cedar Grove Village.

Roaring River Falls is a 5-minute walk from a parking area 3 miles east of the turnoff to the village. Even during summer and dry years, water crashes through a narrow granite chute into a cold green pool below. During a wet spring, these falls are powerful enough to drench visitors who venture too close. Knapp's Cabin can be reached via a short walk from a turnoff 2 miles east of the road to Cedar Grove Village. Here, during the 1920s, Santa Barbara businessman George Knapp commissioned lavish fishing expeditions. This tiny cabin was used to store tons of expensive gear.

Ten miles west of Cedar Grove, in the national forest and back toward Grant Grove, is the entrance to Boyden Cave, the only other cave in the area to host tours. Boyden Cave hosts visitors in summertime only (☎ **209/736-2708**). The cost is $6.50 for adults and age 14 and up; $3.25 for ages 3 to 13. Children under age 3 are admitted free. Tickets can be purchased at the entrance. The cave is open May through October from 11am to 4pm daily.

Cedar Grove also hosts a small village with a store and gift shop, restaurant, laundry, showers, lodge, and campgrounds. This region of the park is often less crowded than others because it is at the end of the road. Remember that it is also closed from mid-November to mid-April.

The **Monarch Wilderness** is a 45,000-acre region protected under the 1984 California Wilderness Act. Part lies on the grounds of Sequoia National Forest and it adjoins wilderness in Kings Canyon National Park. It's small, tough to reach, and so steep that hikers practically need to be roped in to climb. You're near the wilderness area when you pass Kings Canyon Lodge and Boyden Cave.

The **Jennie Lakes Wilderness** is even smaller at 10,500 acres. Although tiny enough to hike through in a day, it exhibits a variety of wilderness features, including the 10,365-foot Mitchell Peak and several wide lowland meadows. This region lies between the Generals Highway and Highway 180, east of Grant Grove.

## 3   The Highlights

**Atop Moro Rock** is one of the most spectacular views in the Sierra. This one shows the Great Western Divide. These high-elevation, barren mountains can appear dark and ominous. Snow caps the ridgeline throughout the year. The cliffs appear towering and steep, but with some peaks over 13,000 feet, they are only slightly smaller than the summit of the Sierra at Mt. Whitney (14,474 feet), which is obscured from view. The walk takes visitors up hundreds of stairs. Take your time. The top offers a narrow, fenced plateau with endless views. During a full moon, the mountain peaks shimmer like silver.

**Mist Falls** is a wide, powerful waterfall accessible only on foot (see chapter 7). It is worth the work. The waterfall is forceful, especially during spring and early summer when it's fed by the snowmelt. The crashing sound of water cascading onto the rocks below drowns out most noises, and there are rainbows galore.

**Crescent Meadow** is a large picturesque clearing dotted with high grass and wildflowers, encircled by a forest of firs and sequoias. The park's oldest cabin is along this route as well. This is a particularly nice hike in early morning and at dusk, when the indirect sunlight allows the best photography (see chapter 7).

## 4   How to See the Parks in 1 or 2 Days

Eighty percent of park visitors come here on day trips—an amazing statistic considering the geography of this place. Three to four days will do the parks justice, but it is possible to take a short walk through a grove of big trees in one afternoon. Day-trippers should stick to Grant Grove if possible—it's the most accessible. Coming from the south, Giant Forest is a good alternative as well, although the trip takes a while on the steep and narrow Generals Highway. Cedar Grove and Mineral King, two other destination points, are farther afield and require an early start or an overnight stay.

If you only have 1 day, we recommend driving from the foothills through Giant Forest to Grant Grove, or vice versa. It's about 2 hours through the park, plus whatever additional time is necessary to resume your route outside its entrances. Start at a park visitor center—there's one near each location and it's a good place to get your bearings. Whether traveling from the north or south, you'll see the varied climate within the park as you pass through dense forest, exposed meadows, and through scrubby foothills covered in oaks and underbrush. In spring and summer, much of the route may be dotted by wildflowers and the southern portion runs along the Kaweah River. This route also passes near two large stands of Giant Sequoias: one at Grant Grove and the other at Giant Forest. Both have easy trails looping through the majestic stands. At Grant Grove, a footpath passes lengthwise through a fallen sequoia.

# 7

# Hikes & Other Outdoor Pursuits in Sequoia/Kings Canyon

## 1 Day Hikes & Scenic Walks

*S*equoia and Kings Canyon are often described as—we said it before, but it's accurate—a hiker's paradise. That reputation comes not because the parks have a network of trails but because of the vast untouched wilderness to explore. There is very little in the way of man-made luxury, but there's a whole lot of nature to soothe the soul. You don't have to hike days into the backcountry to leave it all behind—5 minutes will do. At any place you choose to venture off the paved path, you're likely to find an abundance of natural wonders: colorful flora, fauna, and beautiful landscape created over millions of years of solitude. Below are suggested day hikes to help you experience the best these parks have to offer. We stongly recommend that you purchase an inexpensive trail map; some trail intersections are confusing, and signs can disappear.

### NEAR GIANT FOREST

**Congress Trail.** 2 miles/1–3 hours. Easy. Start at the General Sherman Tree, just off the Generals Hwy., 2 miles northeast of Giant Forest Village.

This self-guided nature walk circles some of Sequoia National Park's most well-known and loved giants. The trail is a paved loop with a 200-foot elevation gain. Here you'll find the General Sherman Tree, considered to be the largest living thing on earth. Other Giant Sequoias along this loop include the President, Chief Sequoyah, General Lee, and McKinley trees. The Lincoln Tree is nearby. Several clusters of trees include the House and the Senate. Try standing in the middle of these small groups of trees to gain the perspective of an ant at a picnic. The walk is dotted with inviting benches as well. Check at visitor centers or at the trailhead for the trail guide.

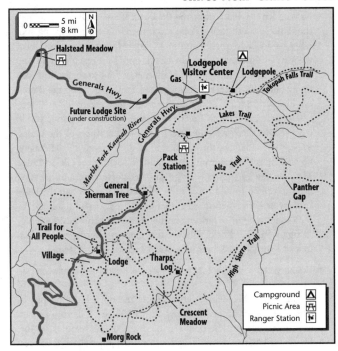

**Crescent Meadow Loop.** 1.8 miles/1–3 hours. Easy. Begin at the Crescent Meadow parking area.

The meadow is a large picturesque clearing dotted with high grass and wildflowers, encircled by a forest of firs and sequoias. The park's oldest cabin (Tharp's Log) is along this route as well. This is a particularly nice hike in early morning and at dusk, when the indirect sunlight allows those with a camera to take the best pictures.

**Hazelwood Nature Trail.** 1 mile/1 hour. Easy. Begin on the south side of the Generals Hwy., across from the road to Round Meadow.

Follow the signs for a good educational walk with exhibits that explain the relationship between trees, fire, and humans while winding among several stands of sequoias.

**High Sierra Trail.** 9 miles/6 hours. Moderate. The trailhead is near the rest rooms at the Crescent Meadow parking area.

This is one gateway to the backcountry, but the first few miles also make a great day hike. Along the way are spectacular views of the

Kaweah River's middle fork and the Great Western Divide. The trail runs along a south-facing slope and is therefore warm in spring and fall. Get an early start in summer. From the trailhead, cross two wooden bridges over Crescent Creek until you reach a junction. Tharp's Log is to the left, the High Sierra Trail to the right. Hike uphill and a bit further on through the damage done by the Buckeye Fire of 1988, a blaze ignited by a discarded cigarette 3,000 feet below, near the Kaweah River. After three-quarters of a mile you'll reach Eagle View, which offers a picturesque vision of the Great Western Divide. On the south side of the canyon are the craggy Castle Rocks. Continue on to see Panther Rock, Alta Peak, and Alta Meadow. At 2.75 miles is a sign for the Wolverton Cutoff, a trail used as a stock route between the Wolverton Corrals and the high country. A bit further on is Panther Creek and a small waterfall. At 3.25 miles is another fork of Panther Creek and above is the pink-and-gray Panther Rock. Follow a few more creeks to reach the last fork of Panther Creek, running down a steep, eroded ravine.

**Huckleberry Trail.** 4 miles/2–3 hours. Moderate. Begin at the Hazelwood Nature Trail parking area, 0.3 miles east of Giant Forest Village on the Generals Hwy.

This is a great hike with a lot of beauty and not a lot of people. It passes through forest and meadow, near a 100-year-old cabin and an old Indian village. The first mile of this hike takes you along the Hazelwood Nature Trail. Head south at each junction until you see a big sign with blue lettering that marks the start of the Huckleberry Trail. You'll pass a small creek and meadow before reaching a second sign to Huckleberry Meadow. The next mile is steep and crosses beneath sequoias, dogwoods, and white firs. At the 1.5-mile point is Squatter's Cabin, a log building built in the 1880s. East of the cabin is a trail junction. Head north (left) up a short hill. At the next junction, veer left along the edges of Circle Meadow for about a quarter-mile before you reach another junction. The right is a short detour to Bear's Bathtub, a pair of sequoias hollowed by fire and filled with water. Legend has it that an old mountain guide named Chester Wright once surprised a bear taking a bath here, hence its name. Continue on the trail heading northeast to the Washington Tree, almost as big as the General Sherman Tree, then on to Alta Trail. Turn west (left) to Little Deer Creek. On both sides of the creek are Indian mortar holes. Some of the largest are 3 feet in diameter and it's unknown what they were used for. At the next junction, head north (right) to return to the Generals Highway and the last leg of the Huckleberry Trail to the parking area.

**Moro Rock.** 0.25 miles/30 minutes to 1 hour. Moderate. Begin at the Moro Rock parking area.

This walk climbs 300 feet up 400 steps that twist along this gigantic bolder perched perilously on a ridgetop. Take it slow. The view from the top is breathtaking. It stretches to the Great Western Divide, which looks barren and dark, like the end of the world. Mountains are often snowcapped well into summer. During a full moon, the view is even stranger and more beautiful.

**Moro Rock and Soldiers Loop Trail.** 4.6 miles/3–4 hours. Moderate. The trailhead is 30 yards west of the cafeteria at Giant Forest Village.

This hike cuts cross-country from the village to Moro Rock. Part of the early trail is parallel to the main road, but the hike quickly departs from the traffic and heads through a forest dotted with Giant Sequoias. A carpet of ferns occasionally hides the trail. It pops out at Moro Rock, and then it's just a quick heart-thumper to the top.

**Trail of the Sequoias.** 6 miles/4 hours. Moderate. The trailhead is at the northeast end of the General Sherman Tree parking area.

This trail offers a longer, more remote hike into Giant Forest, away from the crowds and along some of the more scenic points of this plateau. The first quarter-mile is along the Congress Trail before heading uphill at Alta Trail. Look for signs that read TRAIL OF THE SEQUOIAS. After 1.5 miles, including a half-mile steep climb among Giant Sequoias, is the ridge of the Giant Forest. Here are a variety of specimens, young and old, fallen and sturdy. Notice the shallow root system of fallen trees, the lightening-blasted tops of others still standing. The trail continues to Log Meadow, past Crescent Meadow and Chimney Tree, a sequoia hollowed by fire. At the junction with Huckleberry Trail, follow the blue and green signs north toward Sherman Tree and back to Congress Trail.

## NEAR GRANT GROVE

**Azalea Trail.** 3 miles/1–2 hours. Easy. The trailhead begins at the Grant Grove Visitor Center.

From the visitor center, walk past the amphitheater to the Sunset Campground and cross Highway 180. The first mile joins the South Boundary Trail as it meanders through Wilsonia and crisscrosses Sequoia Creek in a gentle climb. After 1.5 miles is the third crossing of Sequoia Creek, which may be dry in late summer, but the banks are lush with ferns and brightly colored azaleas. Although pretty, azaleas, if ingested, can cause convulsions and paralysis. Return the way you came.

**Big Stump Trail.** 1 mile/1 hour. Easy. Begin at the picnic area near the Hwy. 180 entrance to Grant Grove from Kings Canyon.

This trail meanders through what was once a grove of Giant Sequoias. All that's left today are the old stumps and piles of 100-year-old sawdust. A brochure available at visitor centers describes the logging that occurred here in the 1880s. To continue onward, see the Hitchcock Meadow Trail described below, which leads to Viola Fall.

**Dead Giant Loop.** 2.25 miles/1¹/₂ hours. Easy. The trailhead is at the lower end of the General Grant Tree parking area. It begins near a locked gate with a sign that reads NORTH GROVE LOOP.

The Dead Giant Loop and the North Grove Loop (described below) share the first three-quarters of a mile. The trail descends a fire road and after a quarter-mile hits a junction. Take the lower trail. After another half-mile you'll break off from the North Grove Loop and head south around a lush meadow. It's another quarter-mile to a sign that reads DEAD GIANT. Turn west to see what's left of this large sequoia. The trail climbs slightly as it circles a knoll and comes to Sequoia Lake Overlook. The lake was formed in 1899 when the Kings River Lumber Company built a dam on Mill Flat Creek. The water was diverted down a flume to the town of Sanger. During logging, millions of board feet of Giant Sequoias were floated down that flume to be finished at a mill in Sanger. The lumber company went bankrupt in a few years and sold the operation to new owners who moved it over to Converse Basin. Once the world's largest stand of sequoias, the new company clear-cut Converse Basin. Continue around the loop back to the DEAD GIANT sign, then head back to the parking area.

**General Grant Tree Trail.** 0.6 miles/30 minutes. Easy. Begin at the Grant Tree parking area a mile northwest of the visitor center.

The walk leads to the huge General Grant Tree, which is also the nation's only living national shrine. The walk includes signs to help visitors interpret forest features.

**Hitchcock Meadow Trail.** 3.5 miles/2 hours. Easy. Begin at the picnic area near the entrance to Grant Grove from Kings Canyon.

This trail arrives at the pretty Viola Fall. The first half-mile mirrors the Big Stump Trail described above. From there, hike another quarter-mile to Hitchcock Meadow, a large clearing actually in Sequoia National Forest that is surrounded by sequoia stumps. Notice the small sequoias in this area; these are descendants of the Giant Sequoias logged in the last century. From here the trail climbs

# Hikes Near Grant Grove

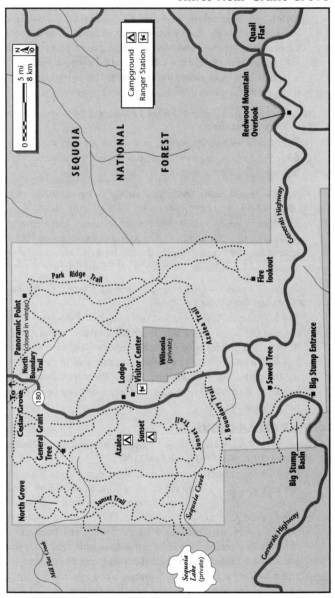

slightly to a ridge, where it reenters Kings Canyon National Park before descending a short series of steep switchbacks to Sequoia Creek. Cross the creek and look for a sign directing you to Viola Fall, a series of short steps that join into one fall when the water level is high. It is very dangerous to venture down the canyon, but above it are several flat places that make great picnic spots.

**North Grove Loop.** 1.2 miles/1–2 hours. Easy. Begin at the lower end of the General Grant Tree parking area.

The trail follows an abandoned mill road from long ago. It cuts through stands of dogwood, sugar pine, sequoia, and white fir. A large dead sequoia shows evidence of a fire.

**Park Ridge Trail.** 4.7 miles/3 hours. Easy. Begin at the Panoramic Point parking area, a 2.5-mile drive down a steep road from Grant Grove Village.

This hike begins by walking south along the ridge, where views of the valley and peaks dominate. On a clear day you can see Hume Lake in Sequoia National Forest, the San Joaquin Valley, and occasionally the Coast Range 100 miles away. Return the same way.

**Sunset Trail.** 6 miles/3–4 hours. Moderate to strenuous. Begin across the road from the Grant Grove Visitor Center.

The hike climbs 1,400 feet past two waterfalls and a lake. After crossing the highway, the trail heads left around a campground. After 1.25 miles, follow the South Boundary Trail toward Viola Fall. You'll reach a paved road where you can head to the right to see the park's original entrance. Return the way you came, or follow the road to the General Grant Tree parking area and walk to the visitor center.

## NEAR CEDAR GROVE

**Bubbs Creek Trail.** 8 miles/5 hours. Moderate to strenuous. The trailhead is at the east end of the parking area at Road's End.

The trail begins by crossing and recrossing Copper Creek. This site was once an Indian Village and shards of obsidian can still be found on the ground. After the first mile you'll enter a swampy area that offers a good place to watch for wildlife. The trail here closes in on the river, where deer and bear drink. At 2 miles, you'll come to a junction. The trail to Paradise Valley heads north (left) while the hike to Bubbs Creek veers right and crosses Bailey Bridge, over the South Fork of the Kings River. Continue hiking east over four small wooden bridges that cross Bubbs Creek. The creek was named after John Bubbs, a prospector and rancher who arrived here in 1864.

The trail will climb on the creek's north side, throwing in a few steep switchbacks to keep you alert. The switchbacks also provide nice alternating views of the canyon of Paradise Valley and Cedar Grove. At 3 miles is a large emerald pool with waterfalls. Far above is a rock formation known as the Sphinx. John Muir named the feature after Egypt's famous likeness. At 4 miles you enter Sphinx Creek, a nice place to spend the day or night (with a wilderness permit). There are several campsites nearby. Hike back the way you came or along the Sentinel Trail described below.

**Mist Falls.** 8 miles/2–3 hours. Moderate to strenuous. Begin at the short-term parking area at Road's End past Cedar Grove Village, and follow the signs.

This is one of the more popular trails leading to the backcountry, but it's also a nice day hike. The first 2 miles are dry, until you reach Bubbs Creek Bridge. Take the fork to the left and head uphill. The first waterfall is not your destination point, although it is a pretty spot to take a break. From here, the trail meanders along the river, through forest and swamp areas, before it comes out at the base of Mist Falls, a wide expanse of a fall that flows generously in spring. There are dozens of great picnic spots here and along the way up. Return along the same route, or at Bubbs Creek Bridge cross over and head back on the Sentinel Trail described below. This will add a mile to the hike. From Mist Falls, you can also continue on to Paradise Valley, described below.

**Muir's Rock.** 100 yards/1 minute. Easy. The pulpit is 100 yards from the parking area at Road's End, along the trail to Zumwalt Meadow.

Okay, so you can't walk too far, don't have time, etc., etc. Well now there's no excuse. This level, simple, short stroll takes you to one of the most historically significant spots in the park's modern-day history. From this wide, flat rock, John Muir used to deliver impassioned speeches about the Sierra.

**Paradise Valley.** 12 miles/7–10 hours. Moderate to strenuous. Begin at the short-term parking area at Road's End past Cedar Grove Village, and follow the signs.

This is a great overnight hike because the valley is so pretty and there's much to explore. But it can also be accomplished as an ambitious day hike. Follow the above trail to Mist Falls and then head up 3 miles of switchbacks to Paradise Valley. The valley is 3 miles long, relatively flat, and beautiful. Hike through the valley to connect with the John Muir Trail and the rest of the backcountry, or return the way you came.

**River Trail.** 5.5 miles/4 hours. Easy. From the Cedar Grove Ranger Station, drive 3.1 miles to the Roaring River Falls parking area.

The trail heads upstream as it hugs the river and can be shortened if you just want to walk to the waterfalls (a half-mile round-trip), or Zumwalt Meadow (3 miles round-trip; a shorter version is listed below). The waterfalls are a quarter-mile along the trail. The falls are short but powerful. Do *not* attempt to climb the waterfalls. Just north of the falls, back toward the parking area, is a sign that reads ZUMWALT MEADOW—ROAD'S END. Take this trail, which initially hugs the highway before breaking off into a beautiful canyon. At 1.5 miles is the Zumwalt Bridge. If you cross the bridge you'll be a quarter-mile from the Zumwalt Meadow parking area. Do not cross the bridge; continue onward up the canyon for another quarter-mile to Zumwalt Meadow. From here there's a slight incline. In a half-mile you'll reach a fork; keep right. The rest of the hike follows the riverbank, which sports plenty of swimming and fishing holes. After 2.5 miles you'll come to another footbridge. Cross over and it's a short half-mile walk back to the Road's End parking area, where you can try and catch a ride. Otherwise, retrace your steps back to your car.

**Sentinel Trail.** 4.6 miles/2–3 hours. Easy. The trailhead mirrors the hikes to Bubbs Creek, the Mist Falls, and Paradise Valley described above.

Essentially what this hike does is encircle a small length of the south fork of the Kings River. After hiking 2 miles on the river's north side, the trail splits and heads north to Mist Falls and Paradise Valley or east across Bailey Bridge toward Bubbs Creek. Follow the eastern trail, but instead of hiking on to Bubbs Creek follow a sign that reads ROAD'S END—2.6 MILES. This will take you through dense groves of pine and cedar, with occasional views of Grand Sentinel. You'll cross Avalanche Creek before emerging into a huge meadow and returning near the riverbank. At 2 miles, you can see Muir's Pulpit, the huge boulder described above. At 2.25 miles, you'll find a footbridge that points back to the parking area.

**Zumwalt Meadow.** 1.5 miles/1 hour. Easy. The trail begins at the Zumwalt Meadow parking area, 1 mile west of Road's End, past Cedar Grove Village.

Cross the bridge and walk left for 100 yards to a fork. Take the trail that leads right for a bird's-eye view of the meadow below before descending 50 feet to the ground below. The trail leads along the meadow's edge, where the fragrance of ponderosa pine, sugar pine, and incense-cedar fill the air. The loop returns along the banks of the South Fork of the Kings River. Grand Sentinel and North Dome rise in the background.

## HIKES ELSEWHERE

**Cold Springs Nature Trail (in Mineral King in Sequoia).** 2 miles/1 hour. Easy. Begin at Mineral King's Cold Springs Campground, across from the ranger station.

This easy loop illustrates the natural history and beauty of the region. It passes near private cabins left over from the days prior to 1978 and the area's addition to Sequoia National Park. The walk offers views of the Mineral King Valley and surrounding peaks. It can get hot and dry in summer, so carry additional water.

**Deer Cove Trail.** 4 miles/3 hours. Strenuous. The trailhead is in the Monarch Wilderness, on Hwy. 180, about 2.7 miles west of the Cedar Grove Village turn-off. The parking area is on the north side of the road.

This hike in the Monarch Wilderness officially maintained by the U.S. Forest Service, starts at 4,400 feet and climbs to 5,600 feet. It follows short, steep switchbacks that climb through bear clover and manzanita. After the first half-mile, it passes above a large spring. Deer Cove Creek is in a steep drainage area at the 2-mile mark. This area is heavily wooded with cedar, fir, and Jeffrey pine. To continue on, see the Wildman Meadow Trail below.

**Kings River National Recreation Trail.** 6–10 miles, depending on distance/ 4–8 hours. Easy to Spring Creek; strenuous to Garlic Meadow Creek. On Hwy. 180, 6 miles below Big Stump Entrance, turn north of a forest service road 12SO1, a dirt road marked MCKENZIE HELIPORT, DELILAH LOOKOUT, CAMP 4¹/2. Drive 17.5 miles to the Kings River. Turn west and drive another 2.5 miles to Rodgers Crossing. Cross the bridge and turn east, following signs to Kings River Trail. The trailhead is at the east end of a parking lot another 7 miles ahead, at the road's end.

So it's a long drive, but after hiking in upper Kings Canyon this is a great place to see what it looks like from the bottom. The views here rival anything in the park, with peaks towering overhead and the river rushing nearby. The hike cuts through the Monarch Wilderness along the belly of Kings Canyon, although this trail, too, is part of the national forest, not the park. The trail starts along a dirt road but soon departs and follows the river, which is broad and powerful at this point. The first mile alternates between rapids and pools that sport great fishing. At 1.5 miles is a view up Converse Creek and its rugged canyon. At 3 miles you'll find Spring Creek, a short but pretty waterfall and good place to rest. You can turn around here for a total hike of 6 miles, or proceed for the 10-mile option. The trail from here ascends the steep Garlic Spur, a ridge that ends suddenly at the ledge of the canyon. The trail above Spring Creek is flecked with obsidian. The nearest source of this rock is the Mono Craters, more than 100 miles to the north. For that reason, many believe this trail was used for trading by the Monache Indians. After the long, steep ascent, the trail heads down to Garlic Meadow Creek. A short way upstream are large pools and wide resting areas. Beyond the creek, the trail is not maintained.

**Marble Fork Trail (in Foothills of Sequoia).** 6 miles/4–6 hours. Strenuous. Follow the dirt road at the upper end of Potwisha Campground, which is 3.8 miles east of the Ash Mountain Entrance. There is a small parking area past campsite No. 16.

This is one of the most scenic hikes in the Foothills area. The walk leads to a deep gorge where the roaring Marble Falls spills in a cascade over multicolored boulders. From the parking area, begin hiking north up the Southern California Edison flume. After crossing the flume on a wooden bridge, watch on the right for a sign to the trail and head east uphill. The trail has some steep switchbacks and is near some large poison oak bushes with stems 3 inches wide. Watch out for these bare sticks in late fall and winter. The trail will begin to flatten out and settle into a slight slope for the rest of the hike up to the waterfalls. Look for large yuccas and California bay along the way. After 2 miles, you can see the waterfalls as the hike cuts through white-and-gray marble, a belt of the rock that is responsible for many caves in the park, including Crystal Cave near Giant Forest. Once you reach the falls, it's almost impossible to hike any further, so don't attempt it. The marble slabs break very easily, and boulders in the area can get very slick. Be extra careful when water is high. This is a good hike year-round, but can be very hot during summer. Upon your return, be sure to check yourself for ticks thoroughly.

**Potwisha and River's Edge.** 0.5 miles/30 minutes. Easy. From the Ash Mountain Entrance, take the highway to the Potwisha Campground. At the campground entrance (which will be to your left) turn right down a paved road toward an RV dump station. Take the paved road until it hits a dead-end at a parking area. Continue toward the river on a footpath to open bedrock.

This was once the site of an Indian village known as Potwisha, home to a tribe of Monache Indians. The main village was just about where the dump station is now (another modern-day reminder of the respect shown Native Americans). On the bedrock are mortar holes where the women squatted nearby to grind acorns into meal. From here the trail continues up the river to a sandy beach and a good swimming hole. The trail turns east upstream before the suspension bridge, then northward up a short but steep hill to the road. Turn west (left) and hike the short distance back to the parking area.

**Wildman Meadow (National Forest).** 14 miles/10 hours. Strenuous. See the trailhead directions for Deer Cove Trail.

This hike through the Monarch Wilderness mirrors the first 2 miles of the hike to Deer Cove. After reaching Deer Cove, it's a steep ascent to 7,500 feet—a 1,900-foot gain in 5 miles. From Deer Cove, hike 3.5 miles to a sandy knoll, from where there is a good view into the rugged canyon drainage area of Grizzly Creek. At 6.5 miles, you'll top the ridge and cross over to the north-facing slope. A quick drop lands you in Wildman Meadow, where a large stock camp occupies the edge of the clearing.

## 2  Other Sports & Activities

**Cross-Country Skiing**   Two Nordic ski areas operate in Sequoia and Kings Canyon national parks. Sequoia Ski Touring (☎ 209/ 565-3435) operates at Wolverton, just north of Giant Forest Village. They offer rentals, instruction, and trail maps for 35 miles of marked backcountry trails. The same company operates in Kings Canyon, in Grant Grove (☎ 209/335-2314). The same services are available here, but the selection of trails is wider. Skiers with their own equipment can ski free. Trail maps are available at visitor centers.

**Fishing**   Easily accessed waters are limited to the Kings and Kaweah rivers. High country lakes have a few non-native trout.

**Kayaking**   The Kaweah and Upper Kings rivers in the parks are not open to boating, but there are companies that run trips just outside the parks. Trips on the Kings are only for the very brave and experienced as it is one of the steepest, wildest rivers in the West.

**Rock Climbing**   There is no rock-climbing school in Sequoia/ Kings Canyon, but Mountain and River Adventures (☎ 619/ 232-4234) teaches rock climbing and can point experienced climbers to the best rocks in the vicinity.

**Snowshoeing**   On winter weekends, rangers lead introductory snowshoe hikes in Grant Grove (☎ 209/335-2856) and in the Giant Forest (☎ 209/565-3135). Snowshoes are provided, but a $1 donation is requested.

**White-Water Rafting**   If you want the thrill without the fear, try white-water rafting. Kaweah White Water Adventures is a local outfit that runs class III, IV, and V trips for beginners and intermediate paddlers. Trips usually last 5 hours, are run in inflatable kayaks or rafts, and are offered from April through August. The cost is $35 to $100 on Monday to Thursday, $40 to $110 on Friday to Sunday (☎ **800/229-8658** or 209/561-1000). Half the fee is due when you make a reservation, but walk-in bookings are often available, too. There are also a few other companies in the area that run trips down the Kaweah and Kern rivers. Call Sierra South (☎ **619/376-3745**), Outdoor Adventures (☎ **800/232-4234**), or Whitewater Voyages (☎ **800/488-RAFT**).

## 3   Exploring the Backcountry

Finding quiet and solitude is not nearly as difficult here as it is in Yosemite. Mineral King and the Giant Forest in Sequoia and Cedar Grove in Kings Canyon are the main points of entry into the backcountry, but the wilderness here is never further than 5 miles in any direction. It surrounds the park and just about any hike that lasts more than an hour will get you there. The park is crisscrossed by numerous trails leading into the high country, including the world-famous Pacific Crest Trail and the John Muir Trail, which begin in Yosemite and end at Sequoia's Mt. Whitney.

Mineral King is a quiet spot that attracts few people because the road to the glacial valley is difficult. Mineral King supports 11 different trails. Avalanches have swept swathes of trees aside and the valley floor is covered with wild meadows. Higher up are woods of red fir, white fir, and lodgepole pine. The landscape is rocky but colorful, with white marbles, red shales, granite, and black metamorphic shale. Alpine trails begin at 7,500 feet and climb from there.

Cedar Grove in Kings Canyon is at the dead-end of Highway 180. From here, to the north and east, the park is inaccessible to vehicular traffic. Hikes from here head out toward the Jennie Lakes Wilderness, Monarch Wilderness, and beyond.

Bearpaw Meadow Camp, a High Sierra camp along the High Sierra Trail, is 12 miles outside of Giant Forest. This tent motel sleeps 12 and provides all bedding and meals. Reservations are taken starting on January 2 for that year and are only accepted by telephone (☎ **209/335-5500**). Reserve early, because the camp fills in a hurry.

## PREPARING FOR YOUR TRIP TO THE BACKCOUNTRY

Be sure to get a detailed topographical map before setting off on any overnight hike. Maps are available at all ranger stations and visitor centers throughout the park. In addition to this book, you may want to pick up a copy of "Backcountry Basics," a free trip planning guide for the wilderness of these parks.

**Permits & Fees** All overnight backpacking trips require a wilderness permit, available by mail, fax, or in person at the ranger station closest to the hike you wish to take. First-come, first-served permits can be issued the morning of your trip, or after 1pm the previous afternoon.

For $10, reservations can also be made 21 or more days in advance, starting March 1. To reserve a permit you must provide a name, address, telephone number, the number of people in your party, the method of travel (snowshoe, horse, foot), number of stock if applicable, start and end dates, start and end trailheads, and principal destination, as well as a rough itinerary. Mail the application to Wilderness Permit Reservations, Sequoia and Kings Canyon national parks, Three Rivers, CA 93271, or fax it to ☎ **209/ 565-4239.** Reserved permits must be picked up by 9am. If you're delayed, call the ranger station or risk forfeiting your permit.

If your hike crosses agency boundaries, get the permit from the agency on whose land the hike begins. Only one permit is required.

For hikes beginning in the Sequoia National Forest, pick up your permits at the ranger district offices in Blackrock, Lake Isabella, Kernville, Springville, or Dunlap; or call ☎ **209/784-1500;** or write to 900. W. Grand Ave., Porterville, CA 93257. This forest wraps around the southern and western portions of Sequoia and Kings Canyon national parks. Permits are free and there are no quotas on trails in this forest.

In Sierra National Forest, permits are also free, but quotas apply from the last Friday in June to September 15. Free permits are issued at the ranger station closest to your trailhead. This forest lies west and north of Kings Canyon National Park. For maps and further information, contact the National Forest Supervisor's Office at 1600 Tollhouse Rd., Clovis, CA 93612 (☎ **209/297-0706**).

The Inyo National Forest administers areas that stretch from the Sierra Crest to Owens Valley. Most trails here have quotas and free permits are required. Reservations are available 6 months in advance and cost $3. They can be made by phone, mail, or fax at Inyo National Forest Wilderness Reservation Service, P.O. Box 430, Big Pine, CA 93513 (☎ **888/374-3773;** fax 619/938-1137).

In addition, food drops can be arranged in advance. You must be there to pick up the food and no packaging from the drop may be left behind. Call the parks' wilderness office (☎ **209/565-3341, then press 1**) for information. Food can also be mailed to the Cedar Grove and Mineral King ranger stations. Packages are held for 3 weeks from the date received, or 3 weeks after the expected pickup date, whichever is longer. Use regular U.S. Mail. Address packages with your name, identified as a trail hiker, with the pickup date all on the first line. Address packages in care of the Cedar Grove Ranger Station, Kings Canyon National Park, CA 93633; or in care of the Mineral King Ranger Station, Star Route, Three Rivers, CA 93271.

The Cedar Grove Ranger Station is usually open daily from 8am to 5pm between Memorial Day and Labor Day. The Mineral King Ranger Station is open from 7am to 3:30pm from Memorial Day weekend to early October.

**Special Regulations & Etiquette**   There are a dozen different regulations for every item that can be regulated, and drawing any consistent warning is difficult. The best thing to do is consult "Backcountry Basics," reservation personnel, or speak with a ranger when you pick up your permit if you have any questions. In general, campfires are prohibited on hikes above 10,000 feet, but this varies as well. Pets, weapons, and all vehicles are prohibited at all times. Stick to the trail and do not take shortcuts. Bear canisters are not required, but are strongly recommended, as the old method of hanging your food from a tall tree limb and counterbalancing the bag out of paw's reach with a rock or stone rarely succeeds in keeping a determined bear from relieving you of all your food.

In a few busy locations, there are limits on overnight stays. There is a 2-night maximum in Paradise Valley and Hamilton Lake and a 1-night maximum at Kearsarge and 1 night per lake at Rae Lakes. There is no camping at Bullfrog Lake, Mosquito Lake No. 1, or Timberline Lake.

## OVERNIGHT HIKES

Be aware of bears that frequent these regions. In the summer months, mosquitoes and sunburn are real problems. Stay off of high peaks during thunderstorms and don't attempt any climb if it looks as if a storm is rolling in. Exposed peaks are often stuck by lightning. And finally, many of these routes are buried under snow in winter. For information on what to bring on your overnight hike, refer to "Backpacking for Beginners" and our equipment checklist on pages 65 and 66.

*Note:* There are 15 ranger stations in the wilderness of the park. There are 7 along the John Muir and Pacific Crest trails. Another 7 are in the southern part of the park in the sequoia backcountry. Most are not staffed from fall to spring. To find which ranger station is closest to your trailhead, consult the park map handed out free at all entrances.

**Alta Peak–Alta Meadow.** 16 miles/9 hours. Strenuous. From Giant Village, drive about 3 miles north on the Generals Hwy. and turn right on the Wolverton Rd. turnoff. Look for the trail at the southeast end of the parking area at Wolverton Creek.

From Wolverton, hike on the Lakes Trail toward the Panther Gap Trail. Head right on the Panther Gap Trail, up through the 8,400-foot gap to Alta Trail. Turn left on Alta Trail; hike past the junction with Seven-Mile Hill Trail and the junction with Alta Peak Trail. Left takes you up Alta Peak, a 2,000-foot ascension in 2 miles that offers spectacular vistas. If climbing isn't your idea of fun, plow straight ahead to Alta Meadow, which also has a nice view and good places to camp.

**High Sierra Trail.** 10 miles/5 hours. Take Hwy. 198 to Giant Village and proceed to Crescent Meadow Rd. Bear right at the Y, passing the signed parking area for Moro Rock. The road ends at the Crescent Meadow parking area.

This trail is a popular route into the backcountry. Some utilize this as a one-way passage to Mt. Whitney. The trail gets a lot of sun, so begin early. From the parking area, head out on a paved trail to the south, over several bridges and to a junction. Turn right onto the High Sierra Trail. You will pass Eagle View, the Wolverton Cutoff, and Panther Creek. Hike at least 3 miles before setting up camp.

**Jennie Lake Trail.** 12 miles/7 hours. Moderate to strenuous. From Grant Grove, drive about 7 miles south on the Generals Hwy. to the turnoff for Big Meadows Campground. The trailhead and parking are on the south side of the road next to a ranger's station.

This is a nice overnight hike that's not too demanding and can be further extended into the Jennie Lake Wilderness Area. From the parking area, cross through the campground and across Big Meadow Creek. From here the trail climbs. At Fox Meadow, there is a wooden trail sign and register for hikers to sign. At the next junction, head right toward Jennie Lake (left goes toward the Weaver Lake Trail) and up to Poop Out Pass. From here it's a drop down to the Boulder Creek drainage area and on to the emerald-green Jennie Lake. This hike can be combined with a second day hike to Weaver Lake. Just retrace your steps to the Weaver Lake turnoff.

Weaver Lake is a relatively warm mountain lake that reportedly is surrounded by blueberry bushes that weigh heavy with fresh fruit in July.

**Lakes Trail.** 12.5 miles/7 hours. Moderate to strenuous. From Giant Forest, drive north on the Generals Hwy. to the Wolverton parking area. The trailhead is on the left of the parking lot as you enter from the highway.

This trail hikes along a string of tarns, high mountain lakes created by the scouring action of glaciers thousands of years ago. Heather Lake and Pear Lake are popular destinations along this route. From the trailhead, go east, avoiding the Long Meadow Trail. Climb up a moraine ridge and soon you'll be hiking above Wolverton Creek, which darts through small meadows strewn with wildflowers. At a junction with the Panther Gap Trail, head left toward Heather Lake. At a second junction you have to choose. To the right is Hump Trail, a steep but always open trail. To the left is the Watchtower Trail, which leads along a granite ledge blasted in the rock with dynamite. With the Tokopah Valley far below, this hike is not for those who suffer vertigo. Both trails wind up at Heather Lake. Camping is not allowed here but is okay further up the trail at Pear Lake. One great incongruity in the wilderness at Heather Lake: the outdoor rest room facilities. However, while it's exposed, at least it's got a beautiful view.

# 8

# Where to Stay & Eat in Sequoia/Kings Canyon

*U*nlike Yosemite, campgrounds here are scattered everywhere, but when it comes to more refined accommodations the pickings are slim. Part of this is because of the planned closure of Giant Forest Village by October 1998. A new lodge will eventually open in the new Wuksachi Village sometime around the year 2000 and will replace guest rooms removed from Giant Forest. You'll find a listing of the noncamping accommodations in the parks in section 1. *Note:* If you're not the outdoors type and you're unable to find a place to stay in either park, turn to the gateway cities or try accommodations offered in Sequoia National Forest.

## 1 Lodging

### INSIDE THE PARKS

If you aren't camping, there are just four places to stay inside the park; two are in Kings Canyon National Park, one is at Giant Forest Village in Sequoia, and the other is in Sequoia's Mineral King. This one will close by fall of 1998. In addition, we've included a section of private resorts within Sequoia National Forest but outside the boundaries of the actual park, such as Stony Creek and the Montecito–Sequoia Lodge. Because of the park's willy-nilly boundaries, visitors actually drive by these en route to various locations in the park. Call ☎ **209/335-5500** to make reservations at Cedar Grove, Grant Grove, or Stony Creek. Other numbers are listed below.

**Cedar Grove Lodge.** Hwy. 180, Cedar Grove, Kings Canyon National Park. ☎ **209/335-5500.** 18 rms. A/C. $90 double. MC, V. Closed in winter.

The motel offers comfortable rooms on the bank of the Kings River. There are communal decks with river views. Rooms are standard motel fare. Getting here is half the fun. It's a 36-mile drive down a winding highway that provides beautiful vistas along the way. It's also above the Cedar Grove Cafe, which is described later in this chapter.

**Giant Forest Lodge.** Hwy. 198, Giant Forest, Sequoia National Park. ☎ **209/ 335-5500.** 83 rms, 1 suite. $109 double; $272 suite. MC, V. Closed in winter and will close permanently in Oct 1998.

Motel-style rooms with either two double or two queen-size beds. All rooms are carpeted with minimal furnishings. There are two restaurants nearby described later in this chapter.

**Grant Grove Lodge.** Hwy. 180, Grant Grove, Kings Canyon National Park. ☎ **209/335-5500.** 52 cabins and rms, 9 with private bath. $40–$80 double. MC, V.

Amenities are in scarce supply at this rustic lodge. Nine cabins have electricity, indoor plumbing, and private baths. The other 43 are cabins with kerosene lanterns for light, wood-burning stoves for heat, and communal bathrooms. Some are rustic wooden cabins; others are made of canvas. Still, rooms and tents provide comfortable places to stay. Some cabins have outdoor stoves for cooking. There's a 30-room, modern unit being added now, which will be ready by fall of 1998. It's also near the Grant Grove Coffee Shop described in chapter 1.

**Silver City Resort.** Mineral King, Sequoia National Park. ☎ **209/561-3223.** In winter, call ☎ 209/724-4109. 15 cabins, 8 with shared bath. $55–$175 double. MC, V. Closed Sept–May. Take Hwy. 198 through Three Rivers to the Mineral King turnoff. Silver City is a little more than halfway between Lookout Point and Mineral King.

This place fills up fast. Reservations are accepted in January for the year. Call the winter line listed above. Most of the cabins have kitchens or wood-burning stoves. Less expensive rooms can sleep two to five people. More expensive units have three bedrooms, private bathrooms, and a living area.

## IN SEQUOIA NATIONAL FOREST

**Kings Canyon Lodge.** Hwy. 180, Sequoia National Forest. ☎ **209/335-2405.** 11 cabins and rms, 2 with shared bath. $65–$150 double. MC, V. Sometimes closed in winter. Take Hwy. 180 from Grant Grove toward Cedar Grove. The lodge is at the halfway point, about 15 miles from both locations.

Built in the 1930s, this lodge is practically a historic landmark. It's also one of the only places to buy gasoline near the parks and uses double gravity pumps that are worth seeing even if you don't need to fill up. The lodge is a mixture of cabins and rooms. All were built out of knotty pine. Each has either one or two double beds. There is also a bar and grill on-site that serves breakfast, lunch, and family-style dinners.

**Facilities:** Nature trails.

**Montecito–Sequoia Lodge.** 8000 Generals Hwy., Sequoia National Forest.
☎ **800/227-9900,** 800/843-8667, or 209/565-3388. Fax 209/565-3223.
36 rms and suites, plus 13 cabins that share a bathhouse. $88–$128 double,
plus $8–$59 for each extra person. Lower rates available off-season. Special
weeklong packages available. Rates include breakfast and dinner. AE, DC, DISC,
MC, V. Take Hwy. 180 into the park, turn right at the fork, and drive 8 miles
south to the lodge entrance, turn right, and follow the road about $1/2$-mile to
the parking lot.

The Montecito offers comfortable rooms in a well-stocked resort
that caters to families with children and large groups. That said, it
also does just as well at providing for guests of all ages. It's also the
only sizable lodge open all year in the Sequoia/Kings Canyon area.
The lodge itself is in Sequoia National Forest, between Grant Grove
and Lodgepole. Rooms are located in four separate buildings. Another 13 individual cabins share a bathhouse. The main building
and many private rooms overlook the Kaweah Range. Meals are
served buffet style. There is also a bar on the premises. A large lake
accommodates sailing and canoeing. During winter, guests can also
go cross-country skiing, snowshoeing, and ice-skating.

**Facilities:** Large heated outdoor pool, Jacuzzi, sundeck, two outdoor tennis courts, water-sports equipment, nature trails, game
room, children and teen programs, conference rooms, laundry.

**Stony Creek Lodge.** Generals Hwy., Sequoia National Forest. ☎ **209/
335-5500** or 209/561-3314. 11 rms. $100 double. Lower rates available off-
season. MC, V. Closed Sept–May. Take the Stony Creek Village exit off the Generals Hwy. between Grant Grove and Giant Village.

This is the plushest place to stay in the Sequoia/Kings Canyon area.
Rooms are cozy and large. The lodge itself is in Sequoia National
Forest, between Grant Grove and Lodgepole. A restaurant is nearby.

**Facilities:** Nature trails, laundry, tour desk.

## OUTSIDE THE PARKS

Of the two entrances to the parks, Highway 198 offers the bulk of
accommodations. One important note: As the highway bisects the
town of Three Rivers, its name changes to Sierra Drive. The Three
Rivers Reservation Centre offers one-stop shopping (☎ **209/
561-0410**) for guests looking for a place to stay in the Three Rivers and Lemon Cove areas. Visalia is another option, and there are
a few scattered motels along Highway 180 also listed here.

**Ben Maddox House.** 601 N. Encina St., Visalia. ☎ **800/401-9800** or 209/
739-0721. 4 rms. TV TEL. $85 double. All rates include breakfast. AE, DISC,
MC, V.

The house is set on a Victorian-lined street, 4 blocks from down-town. Large palm trees grace the front yard and the house itself is impressive, with a large, triangular gable. Built of redwood in 1876, the owners of the Ben Maddox House have worked to retain the home's original charm. Rooms are trimmed in dark oak with white oak floors. Furnishings date to the 1700s and 1800s. Two front rooms have a small porch accessed through French doors. Breakfast is cooked to order from a menu.

**Facilities:** Swimming pool, Jacuzzi.

**Best Western Holiday Lodge.** 40105 Sierra Dr., Three Rivers. ☎ **800/ 528-1234** or 209/561-4119. Fax 209/561-3427. 50 rms and 4 suites, 3 rms with shower only. A/C TV TEL. $67–$85 double. AE, DC, DISC, JCB, MC, V.

Standard motel fare in a nice location. Most rooms look out on the Kaweah River. Rooms come with two double beds, two queens, one king, or one queen. Suites have a separate living area, two televisions, and sofas that fold out for sleeping. Some rooms have fireplaces. If an agent at the toll-free number says the motel is full, call the front desk directly.

**Facilities:** Outdoor pool, children's playground.

**Buckeye Tree Lodge.** 46000 Sierra Dr., Three Rivers. ☎ **209/561-5900.** Fax 209/561-4611. 11 rms and 1 cottage, 8 with shower only. A/C TV TEL. $47–$114 double. AE, DC, DISC, MC, V.

This lodge looks pretty average from the outside, but its rolling lawns that end at the riverbank are picturesque. This is a relaxing place to stay, with rear porches off of every room. Rooms are standard but come equipped with a refrigerator and VCR. Pets are allowed as well and should be declared when making reservations.

**Lake Elowin Resort.** 43840 Dineley Dr., Three Rivers. ☎ **209/561-3460.** Fax 209/561-1300. 10 cabins, with showers only. A/C. $60–$92 double. AE, CB, DC, DISC, JCB, MC, V. From eastbound Sierra Dr. in Three Rivers, about 2.5 miles before the park entrance, turn left on Dineley Dr. (the street sign says DINLEY) and drive across a bridge. Bear right, and it's less than ¹/₂-mile to the resort's driveway.

Undoubtedly one of the best places to stay in the Sierra, this 70-year-old resort is as a resort should be: a place to get away from it all. No phones, no televisions, rustic but clean cabins nestled under huge trees, all looking out at Lake Elowin, a small body of water above the Kaweah River. Brothers Milton and Dennis Melkonian have owned it for years. Milton purchased it after returning from Southeast Asia with the idea of creating a place to coexist with nature. That was more than 20 years ago, and to hear him talk, there's still much more to do. He is fastidious about his creation. All guests must sign a contract upon check-in saying they'll abide by the rules: no smoking, no littering, no car alarms, no pets, no visitors, etc. Guests who break the rules are fined $150. But they're easy rules to abide by, more in place to ward off those with an uncooperative attitude. This place attracts all kinds: writers, artists, white-collar, blue-collar, teachers, electricians, students. Cabins can accommodate two to six people. Cabin No. 1 sits close to the lake, with a nice view from the kitchen window. It also has a bedroom, ample-size living room, and bath. Cabin No. 10 has a bedroom that sleeps five, a family room, and a dining area. All cabins include linens and towels, kitchen utensils, pots and pans. Some have fireplaces and barbecues. You bring the food, sun block, and good attitude. Visit it on the World Wide Web at **www.resorts@lake-elowin**.

**Mesa Verde Plantation Bed & Breakfast.** 33038 Hwy. 198, Lemon Cove. ☎ **800/240-1466** or 209/597-2555. Fax 209/587-2551. 8 rms, 4 with full bath, 2 with shower only, 2 with shared bath. A/C. $70–$125 double. Rates include full breakfast. AE, DC, DISC, MC, V. On Hwy. 198, 16 miles west of the park entrance.

A cross between the Southwest and the Old South, with enough *Gone with the Wind* theme rooms to fulfill a schoolgirl's fantasies. The rooms are named for characters in the film and we're sure the movie's fans will love this place. Scarlett's Room is more of a bridal suite with a large bath. Rhett's Room is dim and dark, Belle's looks like a bordello (one of our favorites), and Prissy's Room is painted a hot pink apt to cause minor brain hemorrhaging. In striving for originality, the decorator went overboard. Another slightly uncomfortable point: The phrase "private bath" here sometimes means not only will you be sharing facilities with other guests but in several rooms toilets are sequestered behind a curtain, which may provide your roommate with a little more information than he or she needs to know. Visit it for yourself on the World Wide Web at **www.plantationbnb.com**.

   **Facilities:** The best part about this place is the large swimming pool and oversize Jacuzzi out back.

**Organic Gardens Bed & Breakfast.** 44095 Dineley Dr., Three Rivers. ☎ **209/561-3652.** 2 rms. A/C. $104 double, $20 per extra person. Rates include full breakfast. 2-night minimum stay on weekends. MC, V. From eastbound Sierra Dr. in Three Rivers, about 2.5 miles before the park entrance, turn left on Dineley Dr. (the street sign says DINLEY) and drive across a bridge. Bear right again and drive about a mile. The driveway will be on your left.

   This B&B is a tiny jewel tucked into the Sierra. The two large guest rooms are enhanced by the obvious attention to detail that went into their design (for example, both have private entrances and solariums). The tile floors were laid by the innkeepers, rooms are aired out between occupancies, there's a Jacuzzi (guests can request private hours) and photography/looming studio on the premises, as well as an impressive organic garden. The best part of all of this is the hospitality of owners Brenda Stoltzfus and Saundra Sturdevant, who moved here from the Bay Area. Breakfasts are vegetarian and served on the deck, weather permitting. Times are flexible. The menu may include crepes, pumpkin-walnut scones, fried potatoes, homemade bread, and homemade granola with yogurt, seasonal fruits, and fresh coffee. Visit their web site at **www.theworks.com/~eggplant**. The house is nonsmoking.

**Facilities:** Jacuzzi.

**Radisson Hotel.** 300 S. Court St., Visalia. ☎ **800/333-3333** or 209/636-1111. Fax 209/636-8224. 201 rms, 7 suites. A/C MINIBAR TV TEL. $100–$130 double; $225–$450 suite. Additional person $15. AE, CB, DC, MC, V.

A pretty glamorous place to stay, this hotel is 7 blocks from downtown Visalia. The rooms have balconies, room service until 2am, and the suites have stocked bars. The hotel supplies free cribs and free airport transfers. Exercise equipment and bikes are available. There's an on-site restaurant serving all three meals.

**Facilities:** Outdoor swimming pool.

**Sierra Inn.** 37692 E. Kings Canyon (Hwy. 180), Dunlap. ☎ **209/338-2144.** 8 rms, 1 suite. TV. $50–$150 double in summer, $45–100 in winter. DISC, MC, V.

The best thing about this place is its choice location just 11 miles from the Big Stump Entrance to Kings Canyon. Rooms come with either one double or two twin beds, and the suite has a kitchen and room to sleep at least four people. There's an inviting restaurant and bar on the premises that hops in the summertime and serves breakfast, lunch, and dinner. There is no dress code, but dinner reservations are suggested during peak season.

**Sierra Lodge.** 43175 Sierra Dr., Three Rivers. ☎ **800/367-8875** or 209/561-3681. Fax 209/561-3264. 17 rms, 5 suites; 8 rms with shower only. A/C TV TEL. $49–$155 double. AE, CB, DC, DISC, MC, V.

Built to resemble a Swiss chalet, this is a funky place to stay. Rooms all enter from double sliding-glass doors. They're spotless but tend to be snug, and some have fireplaces. All rooms contain a small refrigerator. The bathtubs are tiny.

**Facilities:** Small outdoor pool.

**Spalding House.** 631 N. Encinal St., Visalia. ☎ **209/739-7877.** Fax 209/625-0902. 3 suites. $85 suite. Rates include breakfast. MC, V.

This turn-of-the century Colonial Revival house offers only suites, each with a private bath and sitting room. Guests always enjoy the library that contains more than 1,500 books and the music room with its 1923 Steinway grand piano. The owners have restored the entire home themselves, decorating it with Oriental rugs, antiques, and reproductions. It is totally nonsmoking.

**Town House Motel.** 1308 Church Ave., Sanger. ☎ **209/875-5521.** 19 rms, 15 with shower only. A/C TV TEL. $40 double. AE, DISC, MC, V. Take Hwy. 180 east from Fresno. Turn right on Academy Dr. and drive 2 miles to Sanger. The motel is on your left as you cross the railroad tracks.

The staff is quite helpful in this motel offering clean but spare rooms. The best thing about this place—the price. The worst thing—its proximity to the railroad tracks.

## 2  Camping

Camping reservations for Sequoia/Kings Canyon should be directed to Biospherics, Inc. at ☎ **800/365-2267.** Again, as we went to press, this service was not up and running and was expected to be so as of March 15, 1998. If you are unsuccessful using this number, try the general Sequoia/Kings Canyon information line at ☎ **209/565-3341.** Making campsite reservations is not a huge issue in Sequoia/Kings Canyon, though, because 12 of the 14 campsites in the parks are on a first-come, first-served basis and do not accept reservations in advance.

*A reminder:* You'll need a wilderness permit to stay overnight in the backcountry. For more information on wilderness camping, see chapter 1.

There is a 14-day camping limit in the park from June 14 to September 14, with a 30-day maximum per year. Unless otherwise noted, campgrounds are open year-round. Many campgrounds at higher elevations close in late fall. There is generally a limit of one vehicle and six people per campsite, except at Potwisha, which allows two vehicles. Group campsites are available at Dorst, Sunset, and Canyon View. See the fees and permits section of chapter 4. Trailers are permitted at most of the campgrounds; check listings. There are no hookups at any of the campgrounds. Pets are allowed in all campgrounds, but must be on a leash.

Outside the park, campgrounds can be found in Sequoia National Forest and in nearby communities.

## Sequoia/Kings Canyon Campgrounds

| Campground | Elev. (ft.) | Total Sites | RV Hook-ups | Dump Station | Toilets | Drinking Water | Showers | Fire Pits/Grills | Laundry | Public Phone | Reservations Possible | Fees | Open |
|---|---|---|---|---|---|---|---|---|---|---|---|---|---|
| **Inside Sequoia National Park** | | | | | | | | | | | | | |
| Atwell Mill | 6,650 | 21 | 0 | no | yes | yes | no | yes | no | yes | no | $6 | May–Oct |
| Buckeye Flat | 2,800 | 28 | 0 | no | yes | yes | no | yes | no | yes | no | $12 | Apr–Oct |
| Cold Springs | 7,500 | 40 | 0 | no | yes | yes | no | yes | no | yes | no | $6 | May–Oct |
| Dorst | 6,700 | 218 | 0 | yes | yes | yes | no | yes | yes | yes | yes | $14 | May–Oct |
| Lodgepole | 6,700 | 250 | 0 | yes | yes | yes | yes | yes | yes | yes | yes | $14 | May–Oct |
| Potwisha | 2,100 | 44 | 0 | yes | yes | yes | no | yes | no | yes | no | $12 | all year |
| South Fork | 3,650 | 13 | 0 | no | yes | no | no | yes | no | yes | no | $6 | all year |
| **Inside Kings Canyon National Park** | | | | | | | | | | | | | |
| Azalea | 6,600 | 114 | 0 | yes | yes | yes | no | yes | no | yes | no | $12 | all year |
| Crystal Springs | 6,600 | 66 | 0 | yes | yes | yes | yes | yes | no | yes | no | $12 | May–Oct |
| Moraine | 4,600 | 120 | 0 | yes | yes | yes | yes | yes | yes | yes | no | $12 | May–Oct |

| | | | | | | | | | | | | | |
|---|---|---|---|---|---|---|---|---|---|---|---|---|---|
| Sentinel | 4,600 | 83 | 0 | yes | yes | yes | yes | yes | yes | yes | no | $12 | May–Nov |
| Sheep Creek | 4,600 | 111 | 0 | yes | yes | yes | yes | yes | yes | yes | no | $12 | May–Oct (as needed) |
| Sunset | 6,600 | 119 | 0 | yes | yes | yes | yes | yes | yes | yes | no | $12 | May–Oct (as needed) |
| **Outside the Parks** | | | | | | | | | | | | | |
| Big Meadows | 7,600 | 15 | 0 | no | yes | no | no | yes | no | yes | no | free | June–Oct |
| Buck Rock | 7,500 | 5 | 0 | no | yes | no | no | yes | no | yes | no | free | June–Oct |
| Hume Lake | 5,200 | 40 | 0 | no | yes | no | no | yes | yes | yes | no | $12 | May–Sept |
| Landslide | 5,800 | 9 | 0 | no | yes | no | no | yes | no | yes | no | free | May–Oct |
| Upper Ten Mile | 5,800 | 10 | 0 | no | yes | no | no | yes | no | yes | no | free | May–Oct |
| Horse Creek | 300 | 80 | 0 | yes | yes | yes | yes | yes | yes | yes | no | $14 | all year |
| Lemon Cove | 300 | 55 | 30 | yes | yes | yes | yes | yes | yes | yes | good idea | $15–$19 | all year |

It's important to remember that when camping, proper food storage is *required* for the sake of black bears in the parks. See local bulletin boards for instructions.

# IN SEQUOIA NATIONAL PARK

**Atwell Mill.** Mineral King, Sequoia National Park. ☎ **209/565-3341** for recorded information. 21 tent sites. No reservations. $6. Piped water. Pit toilets, fireplaces, and picnic tables. Open Memorial Day to mid-Oct. From Hwy. 198 in Three Rivers, take Mineral King Rd. east for 20 miles to the campground. No trailers or RVs.

A pretty, small campground near the East Fork of the Kaweah River, at Atwell Creek. Elevation is 6,500 feet.

**Buckeye Flat.** The Foothills, Sequoia National Park. ☎ **209/565-3341**. 28 tent sites. No reservations. $12. Piped water. Flush toilets, fireplaces, and picnic tables. Open late Apr to mid-Oct. From the Ash Mountain Entrance, drive about 6 miles northeast on the Generals Hwy. to the Hospital Rock Ranger Station. Follow signs to the campground, which is several miles down a narrow, windy road.

Another small campground in a park where large campgrounds dominate. This one is set along the Middle Fork of the Kaweah River. This campground offers lots of shade and privacy, but it still gets toasty in summer.

**Cold Springs.** Mineral King, Sequoia National Park. ☎ **209/565-3341** for recorded information. 40 tent sites. No reservations. $6. Piped water. Pit toilets, fireplaces, and picnic tables. Open Memorial Day to mid-Oct. From Hwy. 198 in Three Rivers, take Mineral King Rd. east for 25 miles to the campground. Not recommended for trailers or RVs.

Cold Springs is a beautiful place to stay—it's just not very accessible. But once you get there, you'll be rewarded with beautiful scenery. This campground is at an elevation of 7,500 feet, the highest car camping available in the park. It's also a good starting point for many backcountry hikes, as it's near the Mineral King Ranger Station.

**Dorst.** Giant Forest, Sequoia National Forest. ☎ **209/565-3341**. 218 tent and RV sites. $14. Group campsites by reservation only $15–$50. Piped water. Flush toilets, fireplaces, and picnic tables. Open May–Sept. From Giant Forest, drive 14 miles northwest on the Generals Hwy.

This is one of the larger campgrounds in the park. Set at 6,700 feet, Dorst is also one of the highest. It's near some nice backcountry trails and Muir Grove. A grocery, dump station, and laundry are 8 miles down the road at Lodgepole. There are also evening ranger programs.

**Lodgepole.** Giant Forest, Sequoia National Park. ☎ **800/365-2267**. 250 tent and RV sites. Reservations required late May to mid-Oct. $14. Piped water. Flush toilets, fireplaces, and picnic tables. Wheelchair accessible rest room. From Giant Forest Village, drive 5 miles northeast of the Generals Hwy.

This is the park's largest campground and one of the most popular. It's pretty but crowded. In summer, you'll find nearby a grocery, showers, restaurant, visitor center, nature center for children, laundry, dump station, gift shop, horseback-riding facilities—you name it. Evening ranger talks are held. The campground is near some pretty spectacular big trees and enough backcountry trails to offer some solitude.

**Potwisha.** The Foothills, Sequoia National Park. ☎ **209/565-3341** for recorded information. 44 tent and RV sites. No reservations. $12. Piped water. Flush toilets, fireplaces, and picnic tables. From the Ash Mountain Entrance, drive 3 miles northeast on the Generals Hwy. to the campground entrance.

This is one of the smaller campgrounds in the park, located along the Marble Fork of the Kaweah River. Sites are nestled beneath oak trees, but it can get very hot in the summer.

**South Fork.** The Foothills, Sequoia National Park. ☎ **209/565-3341** for recorded information. 13 tent sites. No reservations. $6. No piped water. Pit toilets, fireplaces, and picnic tables. Take Hwy. 198 from Visalia to Three Rivers and turn east on South Fork Rd. Drive 23 miles to the campground.

The smallest and most remote campground in the park, South Fork is just inside Sequoia's southwestern border. It is set along the South Fork of the Kaweah River. A ranger station nearby has hiking maps and information.

## IN KINGS CANYON NATIONAL PARK

**Azalea.** Grant Grove, Kings Canyon National Park. ☎ **209/565-3341** for recorded information. 114 tent and RV sites. No reservations. $12. Piped water. Flush toilets, fireplaces, and picnic tables. Wheelchair accessible rest room. From the Big Stump Entrance, take Hwy. 180 for 1.75 miles east to the campground.

This is one of the nicest large campgrounds in the park. It's set at 6,600 feet, near the Grant Grove and the privately owned Lake Sequoia (available for sightseeing only). It is also near a grocery, showers, visitor center, and dump station. There are evening ranger programs.

**Crystal Springs.** Grant Grove, Kings Canyon National Park. ☎ **209/565-3341** for recorded information. 66 tent and RV sites. No reservations. $12. Piped water. Flush toilets, fireplaces, and picnic tables. Open May–Oct. From the Big Stump Entrance, take Hwy. 180 east about 1.75 miles to the campground.

Grouped with several other campgrounds in the park, Crystal Springs offers a pretty spot to relax near the big trees. A grocery, visitor center, dump station, and showers are nearby. There are also horseback-riding facilities and evening ranger programs.

**Moraine.** Cedar Grove, Kings Canyon National Park. ☎ **209/565-3341** for recorded information. 120 tent and RV sites. No reservations. $12. Piped water. Flush toilets, fireplaces, and picnic tables. Open as needed May–Oct. From Cedar Grove, drive west on Hwy. 180 to the campground.

This is the third of three campgrounds near Cedar Grove, and the one furthest from the crowds and noise. It opens on an as-needed basis. There's a grocery, dump station, and laundry nearby. There are also bicycle rentals and horseback-riding facilities.

**Sentinel.** Cedar Grove, Kings Canyon National Park. ☎ **209/565-3341** for recorded information. 83 tent and RV sites. No reservations. $12. Piped water. Flush toilets, fireplaces, and picnic tables. Open May–Nov. From Grant Grove, drive east on Hwy. 180 to Cedar Grove Village and the campground.

This is one that can fill up fast. If it is full, try nearby Sheep Creek, which opens to catch the overflow. Sentinel is one of three campgrounds in the area and all are within a short walk of Cedar Grove Village. They tend to fill up quickly in summer, but the Park Service opens them one at a time as need warrants. A grocery, visitor center, showers, dump station, and laundry are nearby. There are also horseback-riding facilities.

**Sheep Creek.** Cedar Grove, Kings Canyon National Park. ☎ **209/565-3341** for recorded information. 111 tent and RV sites. No reservations. $12. Piped water. Flush toilets, fireplaces, and picnic tables. Open as needed May–Oct. From Cedar Grove, drive west on Hwy. 180 to the campground.

Sheep Creek is in a pretty spot, along Sheep Creek and a short distance to Cedar Grove. It opens on an as-needed basis. A grocery, visitor center, showers, dump station, and laundry are nearby. There are also horseback-riding facilities.

**Sunset.** Grant Grove, Kings Canyon National Park. ☎ **209/565-3341** for recorded information. 119 tent and RV sites. No reservations. $12. Piped water. Flush toilets, fireplaces, and picnic tables. Open May–Oct. From the Big Stump Entrance, take Hwy. 180 east about 1.75 miles to the campground.

This is one of three campgrounds near the Grant Grove of giant sequoias. A grocery, restaurant, visitor center, dump station, and showers are nearby. There are also horseback-riding facilities and evening ranger programs.

## IN SEQUOIA NATIONAL FOREST

**Big Meadows.** Sequoia National Forest. ☎ **209/338-2251** for information. 15 tent and RV sites. No reservations. No fee. Piped water. Vault toilets, fireplaces, and picnic tables. Open June–Oct. From Grant Grove in Kings Canyon National Park, drive 7 miles southeast on the Generals Hwy. Turn east on Big Meadows Rd. and drive 5 miles to the campground.

A good place to launch a backcountry trip. This camp is at 7,600 feet, set along Big Meadows Creek. Nearby trails lead to the Jenny Lakes Wilderness.

**Buck Rock.** Sequoia National Forest. ☎ **209/338-2251** for information. 5 tent and RV (small) sites. No reservations. No fee. No piped water. Vault toilets, fireplaces, and picnic tables. Open June–Oct. From Grant Grove in Kings Canyon National Park, drive 7 miles southeast on the Generals Hwy. Turn east on Big Meadows Rd. and drive 4 miles to the campground.

A high-elevation primitive camp slightly off the beaten path and a great find if park campgrounds are full or you're tired of battling the crowds.

**Hume Lake.** Sequoia National Forest. ☎ **209/338-2251** for information. 40 tent and RV sites. No reservations. $12. Piped water. Flush toilets, fireplaces, and picnic tables. Open May–Sept. From Grant Grove in Kings Canyon National Park, drive 6 miles northeast on Hwy. 180 to Hume Lake Rd. Turn south and drive 3 miles to the lake.

One of the best places to camp in the area. Set on the banks of Hume Lake, which offers fishing in spring and early summer, and near the Grant Grove of sequoias. A grocery is nearby.

**Landslide.** Sequoia National Forest. ☎ **209/338-2251** for information. 9 tent sites; 3 can accommodate small RVs. No reservations. No fee. No piped water. Vault toilets, fireplaces, and picnic tables. Open May–Oct. From Grant Grove in Kings Canyon National Park, drive 6 miles northeast on Hwy. 180 to Hume Lake Rd. Turn south and drive 7 miles around Hume Lake and up Ten Mile Rd. to the campground.

A hidden gem discovered so far by a handful of solitary souls. The campground is set along Ten Mile Creek and is 2 miles from Hume Lake. There's a grocery nearby.

**Upper Ten Mile.** Sequoia National Forest. ☎ **209/338-2251** for information. 10 tent and RV sites. No reservations. No fee. No piped water. Vault toilets, fireplaces, and picnic tables. Open May–Oct. From Grant Grove in Kings Canyon National Park, drive 6 miles northeast on Hwy. 180 to Hume Lake Rd. Turn south and drive 8 miles around Hume Lake and up Ten Mile Rd. to the campground.

One of two small primitive campgrounds set along Ten Mile Creek, this one is 4 miles from Hume Lake. A grocery is nearby.

## NEAR THE PARKS

**Horse Creek Recreation Area.** Lemon Cove. ☎ **209/561-3155** for information. 80 tent and RV sites. No reservations. $14 and up. Piped water. Flush toilets, fireplaces, and picnic tables. Some sites are wheelchair accessible. From Visalia, drive east 25 miles on Hwy. 198 to the campground.

The campground is on the lake's south shore. In the summer, everyone takes advantage of the cool water to break the heat. Jet-skiers and boaters often dominate the lake. This campground also has showers. A grocery, laundry, and water-sports equipment rental shop is nearby.

**Lemon Cove–Sequoia.** Lemon Cove. ☎ **209/597-2346.** 55 tent and RV sites. $15–$19. Piped water. Flush toilets, fireplaces, and picnic tables. From Visalia, drive east on Hwy. 198, 8 miles past where it intersects with Hwy. 65, to the campground entrance.

This is a KOA campground near Lake Kaweah. Groceries, a dump station, showers, laundry, swimming pool, playground, cable TV, and partial hookups are available. Water-sports equipment is available for rent.

## 3　Where to Eat

Places to eat in Sequoia and Kings Canyon are few and far between—even more rare is finding a diner or restaurant in the park that serves something besides mediocre fare. For the most part, the new concessioner has improved food. Restaurants dish up eggs and cereal for breakfast, sandwiches and burgers for lunch, and a very limited dinner selection. Entrees change nightly depending on the chef's preference, what's available, and demand—factors that make reviewing the food a difficult task. The Grant Grove Restaurant pushes the envelope a bit. The sole "gourmet" restaurant is near Stony Creek in Sequoia National Forest, between Giant Forest and Grant Grove. Keep in mind that all the restaurants in the Giant Forest Village will close for good in October 1998.

Toward the end of this chapter, you'll find listings of places to dine in gateway cities near the park. Following that, there's a selection of markets in the park that carry picnic, camping, and backcountry supplies.

### IN THE PARK

**Cedar Grove Cafe.** Cedar Grove, Kings Canyon National Park. Breakfast and lunch $4–$6, dinner $6–$12. MC, V. Daily 8am–8pm. Closed Oct–May. AMERICAN.

From May through September, this is a fine place to grab a quick bite. The menu is simple and the prices are affordable by national park standards. Breakfasts include eggs, cereals, fruit, and pastries, and lunch is mostly burgers and sandwiches. Dinner features specials that rotate nightly and may include pasta and chicken. There's a nice outdoor seating area near the river.

**Fireside Pizza.** Giant Forest, Sequoia National Park. Pizza and calzone $8–$16. MC, V. Daily 11am–10pm. Closes permanently in Oct 1998. PIZZA.

Specialties include your basic pizza and calzones. Nothing too fancy, but enough to satisfy the craving for a pie.

**Giant Forest Village Cafeteria.** Giant Forest, Sequoia National Park. Entrees $4–$10. MC, V. May–Sept daily 7am–9pm; frequently closes earlier in winter. Closes permanently in Oct 1998. CAFETERIA.

All meals are served cafeteria style. A good place to bring the kids with a wide selection of munchables and a very laid-back atmosphere. Breakfasts include cereals, egg and meat dishes, fruit, and pastries. Lunch is burgers, sandwiches, salads, and rotating hot entrees. Dinner selections include three rotating entrees.

**Grant Grove Restaurant.** Grant Grove, Kings Canyon National Park. Breakfast and lunch $4–$6, dinner $8–$20. MC, V. May–Sept daily 7am–10pm, Sept–May daily 7am–8pm. AMERICAN.

It's nothing fancy or spectacular, but if you're hungry this is the place. It offers a simple menu with something for everyone. Breakfast ranges from omelets and pancakes to simple cereal or fruit. Lunch offers sandwiches, hot entrees, and an all-you-can-eat buffet. Dinner meals include New York steak, chicken cordon bleu, and nightly specials. There's also a tasty dinner buffet available. Prices are a little steep but lower than most national park restaurants.

**Kings Canyon Lodge Bar and Grill.** Hwy. 180, Sequoia National Forest. ☎ **209/335-2405.** Weekend barbecue dinners $6–$12. MC, V. Daily 8am–8pm. Sometimes closed in winter, so call ahead. AMERICAN.

This place tucked off the road between Grant Village and Cedar Grove is privately owned. The restaurant is a short-order fare for breakfast, with burgers, soups, and salads for lunch and dinner. All the food is prepared in a small kitchen and served piping hot. On weekends, try the barbecue dinner special for $12. It includes all the trimmings and is a sort of tradition. The actual dining room here is tiny, and an antique bar occupies the main portion of the lodge. The atmosphere is very kid-friendly around mealtime.

**Lodgepole Deli & Pizza.** Lodgepole, Sequoia National Park. Breakfast, lunch, and dinner $4–$12. MC, V. Daily 8am–8pm. DELI/PIZZA.

One of the few year-round places to grab a quick sandwich, salad, calzone, or pizza. Ice-cream dishes are available.

**Stony Creek Restaurant.** Generals Hwy., Sequoia National Forest. ☎ **209/565-3909.** Reservations suggested. Breakfast and lunch $5–$10, dinner $8–$22. Daily 7am–3pm and 5–9pm. MC, V. AMERICAN.

This is the nicest restaurant nearby and the closest you'll get to fine dining without traveling to Visalia or Fresno. All three meals are available. Breakfast includes the staples, plus a variety of delicious homemade muffins. Salads and sandwiches are served for lunch, and the dinner specials change nightly.

## NEAR THE PARKS

**Michael's on Main.** 123 W. Main St., Visalia. ☎ **209/635-2686.** Reservations required. Entrees $15–$22. AE, DC, MC, V. Mon–Thurs 11am–3pm and 5–10pm, Fri 11am–3pm and 5–11pm, Sat 5–11pm. CALIFORNIAN.

The great debate in the town of Visalia is whether Michael's or Vintage Press (see below) serves better food. Main dishes here at Michael's range from fresh seafood to grilled items, such as pork tenderloin with a sauce of port and wild mushrooms, or filet of rabbit. There are also several good pastas.

**Noisy Water Cafe.** 41775 Sierra Dr., Three Rivers. ☎ **209/561-4517.** Breakfast and lunch $4–$7, dinner $8 and up. AE, MC, V. Daily 6:30am–10pm in summer, 6:30am–9pm in winter. AMERICAN.

A great place to eat. Prices are reasonable and the food is high quality, but the best part about this cafe is the selection. Breakfasts include a choice of omelets, pancakes, French toast, steak and eggs, or south-of-the-border specialties. Lunch includes dozens of hot and cold sandwiches. And dinner entrees include fish, pasta, beef, and chicken specialties, plus vegetarian dishes. The restaurant also has an extensive wine and beer selection and offers a $140 bottle of champagne should you be in the mood to celebrate. There is a large main dining room and a smaller anteroom with huge windows overlooking the Kaweah River. The service is friendly, fast, and knowledgeable.

**Squaw Valley Restaurant.** 30910 Hwy. 180, Squaw Valley. ☎ **209/332-2011.** $3–$7. AE, DISC, MC, V. Daily 7am–2pm; Tues–Sun 2–9pm. AMERICAN.

This restaurant gets the area's best-buy award—meals are inexpensive if not downright cheap, and the portions are healthy. Breakfasts include a selection of special egg scrambles, omelets, griddle selections, and steak and eggs. Most entrees come with potatoes, biscuits and gravy or toast. Lunch and dinner selections include hamburgers, barbecued beef, burritos and tacos, salads, and club sandwiches. Everything is quite good. The atmosphere is diner-esque and the staff is friendly, patient, and helpful. This place doubles as a stained-glass gallery for a local artist, whose works (most for sale) hang in the windows.

**Vintage Press.** 216 N. Willis St., Visalia. ☎ **209/733-3033.** Reservations recommended. Main courses $12–$25. AE, CB, DC, MC, V. Mon–Thurs 11:30am–2pm and 6–10pm, Fri–Sat 11:30am–2pm and 6–11pm. AMERICAN/ CONTINENTAL.

This is the best place to eat within 100 miles. The interior was designed to replicate a gin mill in Gold Rush San Francisco. The bar was imported from that city and made by Brunswick of bowling alley fame. This place seats 250 amid a host of antiques and leaded mirrors. The menu features a dozen meat and fish selections, including steak, red snapper with lemon, almonds, and capers, and pork tenderloin with Dijon mustard, red chile, and honey. The menu also includes ambitious daily selections. A live piano player twinkles the keys in the bar from 5 to 9pm on Thursday to Saturday.

## FOR PICNIC & CAMPING SUPPLIES

Markets throughout the park may have that forgotten flashlight, tarp, or lantern mantle—then again, they may not. It's very hit and miss in the parks, but persistence pays off. Some also have limited backcountry equipment, and of course, bear canisters.

The **Cedar Grove Market** is open 7am to 8pm daily from May to September; closed September to May. The **Grant Grove Market** is open 8am to 9pm May to September and 8am to 7pm September to May. The **Giant Forest Market** is open 8am to 8pm May to September, but will close for good in October 1998. The **Lodgepole Market,** which has the widest selection available, is open 8am to 8pm May to September. During the winter in Sequoia, a small variety of goods is available at Wolverton.

# 9

# A Nature Guide to Yosemite & Sequoia/Kings Canyon National Parks

*Y*osemite and Sequoia/Kings Canyon are parks in transition. Both have long been geologic wonderlands, rarities that recently ran headlong into a myriad of social concerns and natural disasters. Now, park enthusiasts, rangers, and the National Park Service are all taking a serious look at the parks' futures.

## 1 The Landscape

Towering sheets of granite. Lush forests that give way to emerald meadows covered with blankets of wildflowers. Views that stretch longer than some countries and look like the edge of the world. The landscape throughout these parks is incredible. While Yosemite has its almost bizarre conglomeration of sheer granite monoliths and wide-open spaces, Sequoia/Kings Canyon has trees as wide at the base as some homes and wildflowers in almost every patch of sun. All of this comes from the geology of the area, which in itself is an amazing story.

About 300 million years ago, layers of sediment that had been building up on the ocean floor were forced under the emerging North American continent. The process created such intense heat that the sediment turned into molten lava (magma), which then rose up through the continent into volcanoes. Where it chilled and hardened before reaching the surface it created huge slabs of granite. This process continued intermittently for about 150 million years and formed a large mountain range, roughly parallel to the West Coast. That range today is the Sierra Nevada. It is thought that originally some mountains in the range rose to 13,000 feet. For the next 55 million years, erosion was at work. Wind and water ate away at the volcanoes and sedimentary rock, sweeping it out into California's Central Valley. What remained afterward was a Sierra Nevada of exposed granite only several thousand feet high.

Scientists then believe that 25 million years ago earthquakes along the present-day San Andreas Fault began forcing the eastern edge of a landmass beneath the Sierra upward. This mass eventually tipped west, raising tall mountain peaks. This time, without the cover of sedimentary rock, the mountain range appeared more awesome. In Yosemite, the upheaval raised the park's eastern range to a height of 11,000 feet and in Sequoia/Kings Canyon it created the ominously barren and beautiful Kaweah Ridge, also known as the Great Western Divide, a string of peaks amid the Sierra.

The course of rivers raging through the valleys continued to carve deeper, eroding at the bedrock. Great canyons were formed, and when the earth's temperature cooled 2 to 3 million years ago glaciers covered the Sierra Nevada. These fields of ice filled the canyons. Half of Yosemite, it is believed, was under ice. The glaciers tore at the granite, expanding and contracting with such force that they carved deep valleys. The power of this ice carved the canyons steeper than a usual V shape, slicing granite walls vertically into a U shape of Yosemite Valley, Kings Canyon, and smaller canyons in both parks, such as the Lyell Fork of the Tuolumne Canyon in Yosemite National Park.

Scientists estimate 10 glaciations occurred, the last ending between 15,000 and 20,000 years ago. When the temperature of the earth warmed, the glaciers melted. Behind they left steep mountains, smoothed by ice, and piles of debris that dammed the flow of rivers and created lakes in the valleys. The valleys acted as giant bathtubs, draining the melting glaciers from above into lakes that covered the valley floors. These phenomena created Yosemite Valley and the smaller but equally picturesque valley of Kings Canyon. The rest of the landscaping happened in an evolutionary blink of an eye. Over the course of 10,000 years, sediment swept down from above filled these lakes. Meadows formed, then came wildflowers, followed by trees and eventually people who wear black socks with white sneakers.

You can still see glaciers in Yosemite, up near Tuolumne Meadows. Check out Mt. Lyell, Mt. Dana, and Mt. Maclure. The glaciers here were probably formed 2,500 years ago and are quickly receding.

Glaciers are responsible for the variety of rock formations in these parks. There are spires, domes, sheets, and arches. Yosemite has a corner on the market for ratio and diversity, offering one or more of each with an easy 3-mile walk. Most of the unusual rock landmarks were created by fractures within the rock. These occur vertically, horizontally, and at an incline. Called joints, they represent the

weakest point of a rock and a point that has already been broken.
The type of joint most common in Yosemite and also evident in
Sequoia/Kings Canyon is sheeting. Concentric joints form after years
of increasing and decreasing pressure from overlaying rock. When
pressure decreases, the granite expands upward and breaks or fractures off in sheets. If it didn't take so long, it would be similar to
peeling an onion.

Erratic boulders are another common sight. These are large rocks
originally located elsewhere but transported and plopped in an erratic
fashion. Scientists believe glacial ice moved many of the "erratics"
in Yosemite.

Ridges of rocky deposits are called moraines. These were left behind when glaciers receded. The best place to see moraines is in
Yosemite, en route from Tuolumne Meadows to Tioga Pass.

The most famous rocks in Yosemite are Half Dome and El
Capitan. While Half Dome was probably never a full dome like
North Dome, which it faces, geologists believe about 20% of the
original rock was sheered off by glaciers. It looks smooth and slippery, but the face is actually filled with ledges and ridges, making it
a rock climber's paradise. Similar ridges exist on the dome side, en-
abling hikers to climb to the top. Although it looks small, the top
measures 13 acres. (This hike is described in chapter 4.) Half Dome
is 8,842 feet above sea level and towers roughly 4,800 feet above the
valley floor, depending on where it's measured. It's the highest point
rising above Yosemite Valley.

El Capitan is on the left, or north, side of the valley as you enter.
It rises 3,593 feet above the valley floor and is 7,569 feet above sea
level. Toward the top of El Cap, the slope of the rock actually increases and hangs over the valley floor. Called the nose, it's a particular challenge for rock climbers. Look for climbers on the face, as
well as off to the sides of El Cap. Here's where many experts ascend
and beginners learn the ropes. It takes 5 to 8 days to climb El Cap.
The first climber reached the summit in 1958, after 43 days. The
rock is also home to a pair of peregrine falcons that nest here in
spring and summer.

To the right of El Cap are the Three Brothers, three outcroppings
of rock called Lower Brother, Middle Brother, and Eagle Peak. The
rocks appear to be riding piggyback and were formed by parallel
fractures on an incline.

The Cathedral Spires are directly opposite El Cap, on the other
side of the valley. They will appear before you if you turn your
back to El Cap and look carefully—seeing them can be difficult

because the rock is almost camouflaged by the valley wall beyond. Somehow these and other spires in park withstood nature's evolutionary barrage. These spires tower 1,936 and 2,147 feet above the valley floor.

Another spire, this one known as Lost Arrow, is east of Yosemite Falls, below Yosemite Point. Look for the waterfalls behind Yosemite Lodge. The outcropping of rock to the east (right) is Yosemite Point. Lost Arrow is an independent spire in the same area.

Continue moving east to see the Royal Arches, a series of 1,500-foot half circles carved out of the rock, roughly behind The Ahwahnee Hotel. This is an almost inside view of the exfoliation process that formed many of Yosemite's domes. Here, the material that was once above the arches eroded away, taking pressure off the rock below, which expanded and cracked parallel to the surface. During particularly wet springs, water cascades over the arches in great sheets.

Above the arches is North Dome, the smooth, slightly lopsided dome mentioned above. It rises 3,562 feet above the valley floor. Nearby is Washington Column, a spire with its tip 1,920 feet above the valley floor. Ahwahnee Indian legend has it that a man and woman who lived in the valley long ago fought so often that it upset the spirits. The unhappy couple was turned to stone and separated by Tenaya Creek. He is North Dome, with Washington Column as his walking stick. She is Half Dome, and if you look closely a woman's profile faces northeast. Legend also has it that the streak of lighter rock between her cheek and nose was caused by a stream of tears.

Domes and impressive geologic formations appear outside the valley as well. Most are in Yosemite's high county, en route to Tuolumne Meadows. The most impressive is Olmsted Point, an overlook that gives visitors a chance to see the granite Tenaya Canyon. The overlook is 9 miles west of Tuolumne Meadows. From here careful observers can see Clouds Rest and the back side of Half Dome.

Tuolumne Meadows itself is also ringed with domes and peaks, many of which can be more easily climbed than the ones rising above the valley.

There are far fewer easily accessible geologic wonders in Sequoia and Kings Canyon national parks (but there are a whole lot of trees, which we'll get to soon). Moro Rock is a dome towering 6,725 feet above sea level in Sequoia National Park. An outcropping protrudes like a thumb and is accessible on foot. Atop are breathtaking views of the Kaweah Ridge, with some peaks rising 14,000 feet.

Kings Canyon has North Dome, rising above Cedar Grove. Some people with a vivid imagination say it resembles Half Dome.

Waterfalls hang over the Yosemite Valley like a sparkling diamond necklace. The valley boasts three of the world's tallest. Upon entering you'll spot the 620-foot Bridalveil Fall first. It looks large, but that's because you haven't seen the rest of the cast.

The real biggie is Yosemite Falls, located behind Yosemite Lodge. The fall appears as one drop but is a set of two waterfalls that combined measure 2,425 feet. Lower Yosemite Fall drops 320 feet, while Upper Yosemite Fall descends 1,430 feet. A cascade in the middle makes up the difference.

To the left of El Capitan you'll see Ribbon Fall, which drops an uninterrupted 1,612 feet to the valley floor and often dries up in summer.

The longest single fall in Yosemite is Sentinel Fall. It drops 2,000 feet from the west side of Sentinel Rock, which is directly across the valley floor from Yosemite Falls. To view this waterfall, walk back toward El Cap: It's one of the geology-obscured views in the park.

Up valley, you'll find a series of dramatic staircase falls accessible only on foot. These two, Vernal and Nevada falls, are distinct waterfalls but occur just a half-mile apart along the same river.

Waterfalls in Sequoia/Kings Canyon are less numerous but still impressive. Mist Falls in Kings Canyon is beautiful but requires a 4-mile hike. (All hikes for Sequoia/Kings Canyon are described in chapter 7.) This wide waterfall near Cedar Grove is up a rushing creek, which includes several large cascades.

Below is Roaring River Falls, a length of waterfall also accessible only on foot, which flows from Cloud and Deadman canyons. Garlic Falls, in the Monarch Wilderness area just outside Kings Canyon, can be safely viewed from the Yucca Point overlook on Highway 180.

*A note on waterfalls:* Many are fed by snowmelt and rely on winter runoff to survive. In late summer, many of these (including Yosemite Falls) dry up.

## 2  The Flora

There are more than 1,500 types of plants in Yosemite and Sequoia/Kings Canyon, and describing them all could fill this book. With species ranging from tiny lichen to Giant Sequoias, the flora in both parks is similar, varying primarily by altitude. For instance, Yosemite's lower altitudes outside the valley resemble parts of Sequoia/Kings Canyon, and the high country of both parks is strikingly similar.

The trees native to the region consist mostly of conifers and broad-leaf trees. Conifers have nettles and cones, do not shed during cooler months, and maintain their green year-round, earning the name *evergreen.* Broadleaf trees drop their leaves in fall and bloom anew in spring.

At lower elevations, the two most common pines you'll find are the ponderosa pine and Jeffrey pine (both also known as "yellow pines"). **Ponderosa pines** have yellow-orange bark, needles grouped in threes, and bark scales that fit together like a jigsaw puzzle. The trunk of ponderosa pines can grow up to 6 feet in diameter. The **Jeffrey pine** is similar to the ponderosa but tends to live at higher elevations. The obvious difference between the two is the smell of their bark—the Jeffrey's is very sweet smelling, like pineapple or vanilla.

*Ponderosa pine*                    *Jeffrey pine*

**Sugar pines** grow at slightly higher elevations and can be seen along many hikes. These pines have short needles grouped in fives and reddish-brown bark. Trunks can grow to almost 7 feet in diameter. Mature trees sport very crooked branches. Sugar pines also produce large pine cones.

*Sugar pine*

Pines found at higher elevations include the lodgepole and white bark. **Lodgepole pines** group needles in twos, have yellow-orange bark and small cones. **White bark pines** bunch five needles together and have purple-tinted cones that are sticky. These pines tend to be smaller and closer to the tree line.

*Lodgepole pine*

Other conifers of note include firs. Look for **red firs,** with short needles that curl up and cones ranging from 5 to 8 inches. These grow at elevations of 6,000 to 9,000 feet. **White firs** are found lower, about 3,500 to 8,000 feet. They have 2-inch needles that grow in twists off the branch, grayish bark, and 3- to 5-inch cones. Old trunks frequently form large cavities at the base and are used by wildlife as refuges. Both firs grow in forests near Yosemite's Glacier Point and in the Yosemite high country along Tioga Road. White firs can be seen throughout Sequoia/Kings Canyon.

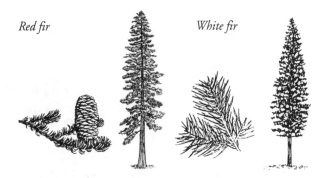

*Red fir*          *White fir*

At the highest elevations (9,000 to 14,000 feet), look for **foxtail pines,** gnarled trees that have adapted to the harsh rocky life of living at the top. This pine, like the white-bark pine, looks stunted and warped. The trunks are usually twisted, the tops spiky and dead looking. Roots grow over granite and the trees make use of a short growing season, allowing them to cling to a frigid existence.

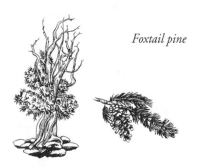

*Foxtail pine*

The uncommon **California nutmeg** is a tree that resembles a fir, with sharp single needles, and can be found in Sequoia National Park, along the Marble Fork Trail, as the hike nears a creek flowing over marble slabs. **Incense-cedar** is often confused with the giant sequoias, as both have reddish shaggy bark that almost crumbles to the touch. But an incense-cedar has flat sprays of foliage that emit a fragrant smell in warm weather, and small reddish-brown cones that resemble a duck's bill when opened.

*Incense-cedar*

Finally, the **Giant Sequoia.** Smaller ones can be hard to identify, but there is no mistaking a mature 250-foot tree dating back 2,000 to 3,000 years. These trees grow to a height of 311 feet, weigh 2.7 million pounds, and can have a base 40 feet in diameter. Tree limbs can reach 8 feet in diameter. The trees are bare until about 100 to 150 feet up, and then branches begin. The bark, naturally fire resistant, ranges from 4 to 24 inches thick. These trees are resistant to decay and each produces small cones of 2 to 3 inches. Cones are abundant and produce hundreds of seeds the size of oatmeal flakes each year, but it takes a fire to dry the cones out enough to release seeds.

*Giant sequoia*

Giant Sequoias can be found at elevations ranging from 5,000 to 7,500 feet, and occasionally as low as 3,500 feet. Obviously, the best place to see these trees is throughout Sequoia and Kings Canyon national parks. The large stands of Giant Forest, Cedar Grove, and Grant Grove offer fantastic, easily accessible examples of Giant Sequoias, and there are other groves, accessible by foot, scattered throughout the park. There are also three stands of Giant Sequoias in Yosemite—the Mariposa Grove near Wawona, and the smaller Tuolumne and Merced groves near the Big Oak Flat Entrance.

Broadleaf trees in the area include the **California black oak,** which grows at lower elevations in both parks. The dark gray to black bark of these trees is distinctive. They also produce acorns and can grow to a height of 75 feet. **Blue oaks** lose their leaves in fall. They can be found in the foothills of between 1,000 and 5,000 feet. Holly-like evergreen leaves can distinguish the **canyon live oak,** the other common oak tree in the region.

*Canyon live oak*

The **Pacific dogwood** produces blooms with whitish-green flowers each spring. The **quaking aspen** has paper-thin white bark and an army of small leaves that rustle in the slightest wind. Along streams and rivers at lower elevations look for cottonwoods, willows, and alders.

Wildflowers and flowering plants bloom in an array of colors in both parks. During spring and summer, nature's bouquets bloom in cracks and crevices, filling fields and meadows. The blooming season begins in February in the lowlands and lasts into early fall in the high country. Much of this is due to the elevation of the parks, which provide a variable climate able to support many plants. The list of wildflowers found in these parks is intimidating and includes more than 50 species, not all of which are included here.

Splashed on meadows and along hillsides is a lavender flower, **lupine.** It's easily recognized by palmate leaves, or leaves that originate from a central point, like fingers from a hand. Look for these along valley floors and in the Wawona region of Yosemite. You will also see **cow parsnip,** bluish-tinged flowers set on spindly stems, with almost fernlike leaves and shooting stars. These dartlike flowers resemble violets at a distance. Upon closer inspection they have an umbrella-shaped top and leafless stalk. Large blue-to-purple blooms that shoot out amid long wispy leaves are **wild irises.** In the Wawona region of Yosemite, look for mountain misery and farewell-to-spring. **Mountain misery** produces clumps of small white flowers atop fluffy pine-looking leaves. **Farewell-to-spring** is a whimsical pinkish flower with four large fragile petals and small, slender leaves.

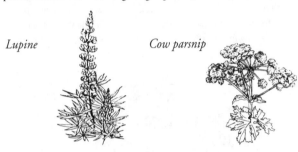

*Lupine*                    *Cow parsnip*

You may also see monkey-flower, showy milkweed and yarrow at these elevations. **Monkey-flower** is one of nature's brightest flowers. Colors range from blue to purple, pink, and orange. The wild-flower grows along streams and at high altitudes on gravelly soil. Petals consist of two-lipped blossoms that more imaginative folks say resemble the smiling face of a monkey. **Showy milkweed** grows in meadows and forest clearings. These plants are sturdy, with large oval-shaped leaves. Stocks are filled with a milky sap, which is poisonous by the way. In summer, the plant bears colorful bunches of tiny five-petal flowers. Later, pods on the milkweed burst and produce a tuft of silky seeds that scatter in the wind. **Yarrow** blooms as a flat, wide cluster of white (occasionally pink) flowers with a pungent aroma. Growing up to 3 feet tall, Native Americans used it as a healing herb, a drink to cure indigestion and reduce fever. Today, the dried flower is commonly seen in potpourri.

*Monkey flower*                    *Yarrow*

At night, look for **evening primrose.** Its flowers have four petals that open at sunset and wilt in the morning. Moths pollinate this flower. Blossoms range from white to yellow and pink, and have a sweet lemon smell. Stems can reach 6 feet in length.

*Evening primrose*

One of the last flowers of the season is **meadow goldenrod,** which grows during late summer and fall. The plant grows in long stalks, with narrow leaves protruding all the way up. It may be topped by a shock of yellow, almost like a feather. The plant is often mistakenly blamed for the onset of hayfever season, but that dubious distinction lies with ragweed. Goldenrod was used by Indians to cure all sorts of ailments.

*Meadow goldenrod*

In forests you'll find pussy paws and snow plant in the shade, and lupine, the Mariposa lily, and mountain violet in the sun. The **snow plant** has a flaming red or orange stalk, while **pussy paws** have small fuzzy leaves and delicate flowers grouped together to resemble the shape of a cat's paw. The **Mariposa lily,** which blooms beneath pines in Yosemite, is named for the Spanish word for butterfly, which it is said to resemble. Blooms consist of three snow-white petals with dark spots at their base. The long stems give the flowers the appearance of floating and Native Americans used to roast the bulbs of these blooms to eat.

*Mariposa lily*

At higher and cooler elevations, a number of slender blooms abound. The **mountain sorrel** has leaves shaped like lilies and clusters of small pink flowers no bigger than the tip of a fingernail. **Spreading phlox** has pointed leaves that stick out like thorns and broad, flat flowers on top. The **meadow penstemon** produces a group of bright pink flowers atop a single slender stalk. The blooms are arranged like trumpets, pointing in every direction.

*Mountain sorrel*        *Meadow penstemon*

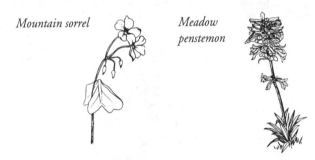

Some more selective wildflowers include fireweed and gentian. **Fireweed** can be found in areas recently burned. It is a quick-growing herb that sprouts with flaming color first among ashes, laying a dense carpet beneath trees. From July to September, spires of four-petaled magenta blossoms top 6-foot-tall stalks, which are lined with delicate leaves. **Gentians** fill damp meadows in spring with bluish-purple blossoms. Look closely and you'll see each petal is edged with fringe that keeps pesty insects out but allows bees in to pollinate.

*Fireweed*

**Columbine** grow in meadows and stake out ground in dry, rocky crevices. A favorite flower of hummingbirds, columbine look quite fragile, with bushy leaves clumped at the base of bare stalks that produce droopy blooms. Their color can vary, but look for five petals that extend backward in a long, pointed tube.

*Columbine*

Shrubs and plants in the park include the wild azalea. They resemble their household cousins and are often first to bloom in spring, spewing forth an abundance of color. The Sierra sports just one variety: the **western azalea,** a low-lying shrub with smooth, deep green leaves and shocks of vibrant color in spring.

**Bear clover** is a low-growing shrub with sticky leaves and a pungent smell. It is also known sometimes by its Indian name, kit-kit-dizze. You'll find this in the Lodgepole area of Sequoia and in elevations around 7,000 to 8,000 feet.

*Western azalea*

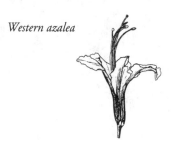

The Mariposa manzanita, with its smooth red-to-purple bark and oval, coin-size leaves, blooms year-round and is but one type of manzanita common in this region. The Mariposa manzanita produces small white and pink clusters of flowers that eventually turn to berries that look like little apples, which is what the word *manzanita* translates to in Spanish. This shrub is plentiful in the foothills of Sequoia National Park.

*Mariposa manzanita*

Now look up into oak trees and search for clumps of green bushes that look as if they were growing from branches. This is **mistletoe.** Despite its holiday charm it is a parasite more than a shrub and grows in green bunches high up in the treetops. This plant sucks nourishment from oaks and many trees. Another pest is **poison oak,** prevalent below 5,000 feet. Look for a shrub with shiny leaf groups in threes and white berries. In winter, though, poison oak stems are bare and very difficult to recognize, so steer clear of any thickets that resemble sticks growing in the ground.

*Poison oak*

Two more worth noting: redbud and yucca. **Redbud** is a flowering tree in the eastern United States, but in California the dwarf redbud resembles a shrub covered with thousands of small petals. Redbud is most common along drier hillsides and along streams. Look for them in the Foothills region of Sequoia. **Yucca** plants grow plentiful in Sequoia/Kings Canyon. A member of the lily family, these pale green, spiky-tipped, desert-looking plants produce a huge, candlestick-like stalk topped with a head of creamy flowers in spring.

*Redbud*

## 3 The Fauna

Think of this as Mother Nature's zoo. There are no cages, no man-made habitats. Only wide-open spaces with enough room for more than 200 species of mammals and birds, all of which are not included here.

The Sierra Nevada is a bird-watcher's paradise. Each year, 135 species visit Yosemite Valley alone. The most treasured feathered friends include the great horned owl, peregrine falcon, and California condor, all of which send bird-watchers into a happy dance. You're more likely to hear the **great horned owl** than see one. This bird's hoots sound like sonar, but it's a nocturnal dweller, making it harder to spot than others. If you happen to hear its hoot, try locating its branch, then look for the bird. It has large tufts of feathers near both ears. But don't get disheartened if you search in vain—these birds are great ventriloquists. You're almost more likely to encounter a pair of nesting peregrine falcons on El Capitan or Glacier Point. For several years now, several pairs have made this their own personal day-care center, hatching and raising their young on narrow ledges before beginning flight instruction. Take a pair of binoculars if you plan to look. The **peregrine falcon** is one of four falcon species in the park. This one is marked by a hood of dark feathers from head to back, contrasting against lighter ones underneath. This bird is a wizard in flight, reaching speeds of up to 200 m.p.h. mid-dive. It is considered an endangered species.

*Great horned owl*

*Peregrine falcon*

Also endangered is the **California condor,** the largest land bird in North America, with a 9-foot wingspan. The birds are able to glide 10 miles at a time without flapping their wings. Keen eyesight allows them to spot a dead animal carcass from miles away. Thousands of years ago these birds ranged as far east as Florida, but by

*California condor*

mid-century they resided only in the mountains of Southern California. Their numbers dropped below 40 in 1975, due to the loss of habitat to building and pesticide use. A pair of condors can raise only one young every 2 years. In the 1980s, the remaining birds were captured and placed in zoos where young were hand-reared. Only recently were some of those now-adolescent birds re-released into the wild—with any luck, some day they'll return to Yosemite.

In both parks, the birds you're most likely to see are the American robin, Steller's jay, acorn woodpecker, northern flicker, band-tailed pigeon, two varieties of blackbird, sparrow, swifts, American dipper, belted kingfisher, ducks, warblers, brown creeper, mountain chickadee, and red-breasted and white-breasted nuthatchers. Yosemite Valley is a great place to see many of these because its environment includes streambeds, rivers, forest, and meadowlands, often within the space of a city block. A stroll anywhere along the Merced River takes you through or within visual distance of all of these birds, whose habitats include the water, meadows, and adjacent forests.

Its reddish-orange breast easily distinguishes the **American robin.** These are the same birds you can see back home throughout much of North America, in suburbs and backyards, building cup-shaped nests on windowsills or ledges of buildings. Before the bird became adapted to urban living, it preferred a woodland habitat. It has long been considered a harbinger of spring, but in reality some of these birds stay put year-round. The **Steller's jay** is one of nature's more annoying birds. Unfazed by humans, it is a bold beggar, landing on picnic tables and elsewhere near food while letting loose a screech that could wake the dead. It's worse when a hawk or owl is in the vicinity. The Steller's jay is bright blue, with a dark head and very prominent crest. This bird is also capable of a beautiful soft warble. Like the Steller's jay, you're likely to hear the **woodpecker** before you see it. Using its beak against trees and branches produces a

*American robin*                    *Steller's jay*

gentle but methodical rata-tat-tat. Woodpeckers can also emit a startling call that sounds like "wack-up." Its black-and-white markings and red crown can distinguish the bird (sometimes there's a bit of yellow thrown in as well). The **northern flicker** is also a woodpecker—look for a brown-feathered bird clinging to the side of trees. Its wings have a reddish tinge and it sports a red mustache. This bird prefers to feed on the ground, where it searches for ants. **Band-tailed pigeons** are like their city-dwelling cousins but prefer tall forest trees to buildings.

*Northern flicker*          *Band-tailed pigeon*

In meadowlands, you'll likely see two varieties of blackbird, sparrows, the black-headed grosbeak, and the uncommon western tanager, a bird with fluorescent feathers. The **brewer's blackbird** and the **red-winged blackbird** both make their home here. Brewer's blackbirds nest in trees while their red-winged relatives prefer slightly marshy areas. Red-winged males have distinctive red patches on their wings. The Brewer's blackbird is, well, black, but females of either variety are drab by comparison. **Sparrows** are small singing birds, streaked by brown feathers and with cone-shaped beaks, whose babies leave the nest at 10 days old. The **black-headed grosbeak** has black, white, and orange markings and a distinctive beak used for cracking seeds. Its soft, lyrical warble is music compared to other

*Brewer's blackbird*                    *Black-headed grosbeak*

valley dwellers, and this bird is considered a sure sign of spring. The **western tanager** is bright yellow with a reddish-orange head that is easy to spot. It's most likely to be seen in Yosemite Valley in spring and summer.

*Western tanager*

If you're near moving water, you might search for the American dipper, belted kingfisher, ducks, and warblers. The **dipper** is less distinctive for its nondescript color and more for its flying acrobatics. Dippers fly headfirst into the river and walk along the bottom upstream, clinging to rocks in their search for food. The **belted kingfisher** is a very visible blue bird that flies low over water in search of prey. You may see it perched above water, clinging to branches and underbrush, and keeping a watchful eye out for insects and fish. It has a reddish band on its chest and a noticeable crest up top. And the call of the kingfisher is distinctive. It makes a loud, rattling, clicking call. **Warblers** are often called the butterflies of the bird world. They are small, brightly colored, and move with gravity-defying ease. Contrary to their name, warblers are undistinguished singers, but they're great at collecting insects.

*American dipper*

*Belted kingfisher*

In forests live brown-creepers, mountain chickadees, and red-breasted and white-breasted nuthatches. The **brown creeper** is difficult to spot because of camouflage feathers that disguise it among tree trunks, which it clings to in search of insects. It is small, with a slender, curved beak. The creeper usually begins foraging at the

*Brown creeper*

base of a tree and works its way up, clinging to the bark with razor-sharp claws. The **mountain chickadee** is another songbird with a delightful melody that sounds like "chickadee-dee-dee." These birds are tiny, friendly, and hyperactive. They have dark caps and bibs, a gray or brown back, and a distinctive white eyebrow. They nest in woodpecker holes or other small tree holes. **Nuthatches** are the birds you'll see climbing headfirst down a tree trunk. No simple feat. Also called upside-down birds, the red-breasted and white-breasted versions are aptly described by their names. The term *nuthatch* comes from "nut-hack," as in the use of one's beak to hack open bits of food wedged in tree bark. They are also partial to abandoned woodpecker holes.

*Mountain chickadee*                                    *Nuthatch*

And let's not forget the **swift,** almost always in flight above Yosemite Valley. These birds spend more time air-bound than any other land bird. When they do stop, they cling to vertical surfaces because their tiny feet are unsuitable for perches. Look up to see swifts flying between Yosemite's great granite walls.

In the Wawona region south of Yosemite Valley are also the bushtit and wrentit, scrub jay, California thrasher, yellow warbler, lesser goldfinch, barn swallow, and the ash-throated and rare willow flycatchers. Many of these inhabit Wawona Meadow. The **yellow**

**warbler** is the more colorful version of its cousin described above. Swallows are streamlined-looking birds with long, pointed wings. They are swift fliers able to eat and drink on the fly. All are migratory and some travel thousands of miles to the tropics each winter. Flycatchers are better known for their insect hunting than distinctive markings. Two of a dozen species, neither stands out dramatically. The **willow flycatcher** is a threatened species. Both have gray, brown, and olive plumage. All are very territorial. The **goldfinch** is sometimes referred to as the wild canary. These are gregarious birds, like the finch, with bright colors and cheerful songs.

*Yellow warbler*

*Willow flycatcher*

Other birds frequently spotted in this region of the Sierra include the bushtit and wrentit, scrub jay, and California thrasher, the last three of which prefer chaparral areas. **Bushtits** spend most of the year in flocks of about 20, constantly twittering at each other with a soft lisping call. These acrobatic fliers are small grayish birds with tiny bills. **Wrentits** are secretive birds, hard to see but easy to hear. They seldom venture far from home and prefer to live in chaparral or scrub thickets. Mated, they form devoted pairs, constantly pruning and preening each other. Close together, they resemble a single ball of gray fluff. The **California thrasher** is one of several thrasher species, all of which have long tails and nest in low thickets. They forage on the ground and are accomplished singers, though not so much as their distant cousins, the mockingbird and catbird.

*Bushtit*

*Wrentit*

The high country of Yosemite and Sequoia/Kings Canyon attracts dozens more birds to its altitude and mountain meadows, including the dark-eyed junco, kestrel, red-tailed hawk, killdeer, Williamson's sapsucker, Clark's nutcracker, and ptarmigan.

**Juncos,** often referred to as snow birds, are common visitors to bird feeders. Small and friendly, these birds resemble the sparrow, which also frequents this region. But the dark-eyed junco has a pink bill, white to bluish underbelly, and dark feathers from the crown down its back. Juncos can usually be seen hopping along the ground in search of food. The **kestrel** is the smallest species of falcon. Like the falcon, it kills prey with a sharp bite to the neck, as opposed to hawks, which kill with their sharp claws. The kestrel is the only species of falcon that raises more than one brood a year, and then only if there is an abundance of field mice and other rodents. The kestrel feeds mostly on insects and small mammals. The **red-tailed hawk** is equipped with broad, rounded wings and a fan-shaped tail. These birds soar effortlessly, using their keen eyesight to scan the area below for prey. The red-tailed hawk is one of the "buteo hawks," like the Swainson's hawk, which prefers open country to wooded areas. The **killdeer** is another performer, feigning a broken wing when intruders venture too near its nest. And no wonder—nests are little more than a shallow depression in the ground lined with pebbles and small stones. Adult killdeer have two black bands across their throats, while chicks have one.

*Junco*                    *Killdeer*

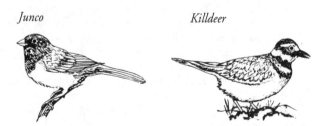

**Sapsuckers** are specialized woodpeckers that extract the sap from trees with their brush-tipped tongues after drilling holes with their beaks. They also eat insects attracted to the sap. The **Williamson's sapsucker** strongly resembles the northern flicker described above, minus the red mustache. **Nutcrackers** are bold cousins of the crow family. **Clark's nutcrackers** specialize in prying seeds from pine cones and make forests their stomping ground. In late summer and

*Williamson's sapsucker*

*Clark's nutcracker*

fall, the birds begin hoarding seeds for winter, tucking them in a pouch under their tongue during transport to less snowy slopes, where they poke holes in the ground and bury their treasure. A single nutcracker can hide 30,000 seeds. More remarkable is the fact that they remember where the stock is buried by the position of nearby landmarks, even when the ground is covered with snow. Clark's nutcracker resembles a crow, with a gray head and body, and black wings tipped white. Finally, the **ptarmigan** is a unique bird well adapted to changing seasons in cold climates. These small, stocky grouse have mottled brown feathers in summer to help camouflage them against rocky mountaintops where they live. But the feathers turn pure white in winter to match the snow. Like all grouse, ptarmigans have feathered legs. In winter, the ptarmigan's feet are also covered with feathers, like slippers. During the spring mating season, males sport a vibrant red comb and strut in short flights while cackling, all to attract a mate.

*Ptarmigan*

Also prevalent in the high country, in addition to the variety of birds described above—Hammond's flycatcher, Cassin's finch, common flicker, pine sparrow, chipping sparrow, white-crowned sparrow, and violet-green swallow.

Mammals in these parks are not as numerous, but for some reason they're a lot more fun to spot. Most common are the mule deer, raccoon, squirrel, chipmunk, fox, coyote, and black bear. At higher elevations, you may also spot the belding ground squirrel and Douglas squirrel, yellow-bellied marmot, pika, pine marten, badger, mountain lion, bobcats, porcupine, California bighorn sheep, long-tailed weasels, wolverine (a.k.a. the skunk-bear), striped and spotted skunks, and northern water shrew.

**Mule deer** in both parks are almost tame. The deer are most frequently spotted grazing in meadows at dawn and dusk. Although they seem gentle enough, mule deer should be treated with the same reverence as any wild animal. Give them a wide berth and, of course, refrain from feeding them. Many injuries have been recorded against humans who attempt to get too close or feed the deer, and incidents of harm are on the rise. The mule deer gets its name from its large mulelike ears. Adults can weigh up to 200 pounds. The deer survive on a mix of grasses, leaves, tender twigs, and herbs. Males grow antlers for use during the mating season. And no, it is not true that the age of a male deer can be gauged by counting the points on its antlers.

*Mule deer*

A variety of members of the squirrel family reside in this region, including chipmunks and marmots. The most common is the **California gray squirrel,** often seen in trees with its gray coat and bushy tail. The California ground squirrel is a brown animal with white speckles that prefers living in burrows. The **Sierra chickaree** is a reddish-colored tree squirrel that chews on pine cones and frequently makes a squeaking noise. **Douglas's squirrel,** common in Sequoia, is an olive to rust or gray color, with a reddish underbelly. At higher elevations, the **Belding ground squirrel** is most easily distinguished

*Douglas's squirrel*

when it's seated—its erect posture resembles a stake driven into the ground. There are at least five different varieties of chipmunks in this region. All are smaller than squirrels. They are quick and love to chatter, almost as if scolding those who venture too near. **Chipmunks** range in color from reddish-brown to brownish-gray, and all have four stripes running the length of their back. At higher elevations is the yellow-bellied marmot. **Marmots** resemble woodchucks. They regularly sunbathe and can tease visitors into believing they are tame. They aren't. Adult marmots appear yellowish-brown, weigh up to 5 pounds, and reach 15 to 18 inches in length. They emit a high-pitched shrill as a warning and live beneath rock piles or tree roots.

*Chipmunk*          *Yellow-bellied marmot*

The **porcupine** is a unique rodent. These short, stock-legged creatures are covered from head to toe with quills that detach at the touch, piercing who or whatever touches them. Each animal carries about 30,000 quills that serve as a serious deterrent to all but the stupidest predators. Porcupines sleep during the day and forage at night, curling into a ball when approached by a would-be predator. In spring, females produce one offspring, which is born with soft quills (thankfully) that harden within minutes. **Pikas** are animals that look like a cross between a rodent and a hare. They are actually distant relatives of the rabbit family. Pikas have oversized ears, although much smaller proportionately than those found on their cousins, and live above the tree line throughout the West in colonies. They scamper over rocks and emit a high-pitched squeal whenever a predator is sighted.

*Porcupine*    *Pika*

**Raccoons** are considered pests in suburbia, but in the wild they are shy nocturnal animals, easily spotted by their ringed tailed and the appearance of a black mask across their eyes. Some are no bigger than a large house cat, but males can grow to 3 feet in length and weigh more than 40 pounds. These animals are adaptive, eating everything from fish and small rodents to fruit, nuts, and earthworms.

*Raccoon*

The parks contain a large number of members to the weasel family. The list includes badgers, martens, skunks, wolverines, and what most people know as weasels. The **long-tailed weasel** can reach 16 inches in length. It is brown, with a white underbelly. In winter, they can turn white but always retain a black tip on the end of their tail. The badger and marten are distant cousins of the weasel. **Badgers** can reach up to 2 feet in length and can weigh 25 pounds. This heavy, short-legged animal has black feet, black and white face markings, and coarse fur that is yellowish gray. The **pine marten** is the variety you'll see in these parks. It's a fast, agile climber that prefers high mountain forests. It is sometimes mistaken for a squirrel, bounding from limb to limb. Actually, it's probably chasing a red squirrel, its favorite dinner entree. If you're not familiar with skunks, consider yourself fortunate. Best known for the awful scent they spray when scared or under attack, skunks are otherwise cute, fluffy animals with distinctive black and white markings. Most common is the **striped skunk,** its white-on-black strip running from nose to tail tip. The **spotted skunk** is more rare, but lives in Sequoia and Kings Canyon national parks. The **wolverine** is one of the largest members of the weasel family, weighing up to 60 pounds. Dark with dull yellow stripes on its sides and forehead, the wolverine, also known as a skunk bear, is much smaller than either a wolf or bear. It is a formidable hunter nevertheless, and prefers to go it alone at high altitudes, relentlessly tracking its prey. It is very intolerant of humans. All members of the weasel family are nocturnal. The wolverine also hunts by day.

*Badger*

*Striped skunk*

Fox, coyote, black bear, bobcat, and mountain lion also inhabit this region. Most avoid crowds and shun humans, but coyote and black bear are even frequently spotted in the middle of Yosemite Valley, where they rely on the misguided benevolence of humans who feed them. **Coyotes** resemble dogs, with long gray fur and bushy tails. They feed primarily on small rodents, and occasionally a fawn, and grow to weigh between 25 and 30 pounds. One of the coyote's most distinctive traits is its howl, a long, haunting call that some consider frightening. The **black bear** is the largest mammal in these parks. It is often confused with the grizzly bear, which is much larger and much more fearsome. Sadly, grizzlies were hunted out of California earlier this century. Incidents involving black bears are more apt to be over improper food storage. Never feed the bears and by no means should you walk toward them. Observe at a safe distance. Despite their names, black bears can also be brown, blond, and cinnamon colored. Adult black bears grow to 250 to 500 pounds, and larger ones have been recorded. They are omnivores, eating both meat and vegetation, and they've proven very adaptable to hot dogs, hamburgers, and cookies. Unfortunately, once they become dependent on human food, these bears can prove bold and determined to continue their new diet. At this point, they must be trapped and killed by park rangers. Therefore, you *must* follow food storage regulations.

*Coyote*        *Black bear*

Foxes, bobcats, and mountain lions are less frequently spotted in the parks, especially the latter two. The most common fox is the **grey fox,** with its bushy tail, reddish-grey coat, and black paws. They are members of the dog family and look larger than they are. Average weight is 10 pounds. Foxes are skillful hunters, and eat rodents, berries, rabbits, and insects. **Bobcats** inhabit Sequoia/Kings Canyon National Park. They are nocturnal and resemble a large cat. Their coat is a tawny color spotted with black. The "bob" refers to their

*Grey fox*        *Bobcat*

stub of a tail, a feature shared with this cat's close relative, the lynx. Adults max out at about 20 pounds, and while much smaller than the next predator on our list, bobcats can kill deer many times their size. They are the master of the slow hunt, methodical, solitary, and patient. **Mountain lions** shy from any human contact, so seeing one is extremely rare and frightening, but sightings have been on the rise in Yosemite. These large cats can reach 5 feet in length. Their fur ranges from tawny to gray, their tails tipped with black. They, too,

*Mountain lion*

are solitary predators who prefer elk and deer but during lean times will chase a porcupine or skunk. The mating call of mountain lions resembles the ear-piercing shriek of a human.

## 4 The Ecosystem

Quite often, the ravages of nature are the forces of change, and such has been the case in these national parks. Recent rock slides and floods seem to have ushered in a new era, one eager to restore nature and do a better job of managing visitors. In reality, preservation efforts and long-term study have been underway for more than a decade, sometimes involving the unlikeliest of partners.

In Yosemite, the return of the peregrine falcon was heralded as a milestone. When bird-watchers counted three nesting pairs and five offspring in 1996, the news traveled across the nation. Several of Yosemite meadows are being restored. It's a similar story with the California bighorn sheep. Years ago, these animals made this park their home. Sheep herders and settlers changed that, bringing disease, competition for food, and hunting. Today, bighorns are again facing imminent extinction.

It's not just animals that are returning. Considerable attention has been paid to restoring meadows, limiting trails, and bringing back native plants pushed out by the impact of humans. In several valley meadows, volunteers planted native vegetation, installed boardwalks to direct foot traffic, fenced off sensitive areas, and removed non-native plants. In some cases, workers had to completely strip sections of a meadow down to bare earth, then painstakingly rebuild what nature intended. The valley has also seen the reseeding of a black oak forest along the bikeway between Yosemite Village and Yosemite Falls. Small plastic tubes stand erect in roped-off areas. Each tube holds the hope of restoration of one of the park's most neglected trees, which were overrun by visitors and overshadowed by taller pines.

Large boulders placed in the Merced River long ago by settlers and early park managers changed the course of the waterway and created unnatural swimming holes. These are being removed, and the river is being allowed to pursue its own direction. Relocating the flooded campgrounds will only assist in this endeavor. Volunteers are working to repair damage done by hikers who step off the tracks, either to explore or to get around water, fallen rocks, or trees. As trails are shored up, these side trips create new, unnecessary ruts that are being eliminated and reseeded.

In Sequoia/Kings Canyon, fire management continues to be a number one concern, along with a host of environmental factors largely at the control of those who live and work outside the park. Fire management has been an issue around the big trees since the early 1990s. Early on, the idea was to preserve the trees, so natural wildfires were squelched whenever possible. It wasn't until the mid-1960s that the National Park Service began conducting research on the benefits of fire, and then only after a noticeable decline in the germination rate of new trees. What it discovered is that fire is necessary and was, before human intervention, common. As noted previously, Giant Sequoias depend on fire to dry out their cones and release seeds. It also burns underbrush and clears openings in the canopy for sunlight to reach the seedlings. In 1968, an unprecedented fire management program began that allows natural wildfires to burn, sets prescribed burns to remove underbrush that accumulates in the forest, and suppresses fires in campgrounds as well as other unwanted blazes. According to the National Park Service, from 1968 to 1989, 156 prescribed fires cleared underbrush on 28,993 acres. Another 410 natural fires were allowed to burn during this time. And over the past 20 years, the regeneration rate of Giant Sequoias has been noticeable.

Other concerns for the park include air quality and drought. Sequoia/Kings Canyon is unfortunately located near California's smoggy Central Valley and has the most chronically polluted air in the western parks. Air from the San Joaquin Valley pushes up against the Sierra. A weather pattern called the Fresno Eddy bounces polluted air down the Tehachapi Mountains and back, where it is trapped in the vicinity of the Kings and Kaweah river basins. Although the national Clean Air Act requires large reductions in air pollution, sulfur dioxide in the air is expected to double in California, causing additional haze. Not only is it disgusting to look at but air pollution is a hazard to hikers, and it has harmed some of the plants and trees in the park, including the black oak, ponderosa pine, and Jeffrey pine. Scientists are looking for ways to clean up the air. Ozone pollution weakens the trees, so that when natural drought comes along, trees, including pines and white and red firs, often die.

Dealing with the issues facing both parks requires time, money, and commitment—all high hurdles to leap. Partnerships have been formed with foundations, nature conservancies, even oil companies, to provide funding for study and restoration. But the single biggest issue for both parks remains overcrowding.

For most of this century, it's been a balancing act between increasing visitation and consistent management. Research has changed some policies and experience is changing others. Education on all fronts continues to strive to bridge the different desires of humans to experience nature and nature to overcome the human experience.

# Index

See also separate Accommodations and Restaurants indexes, below.

## ACCOMMODATIONS

## RESTAURANTS